Acclaim for

"With its mix of high school, space aliens, and conspiracy theories, Lewis' first book in the C.H.A.O.S. series is *I Am Number Four* (2010) for a slightly younger set. . . . Mechanical spiders, jet packs, Nazi/alien alliances, and characters with names like Borog and Zandarr will render certain readers putty in Lewis' capable hands."

—BOOKLIST

"[*Invasion*] draws readers into the action-packed world of Colt and his friends. The narrative presents several well-defined characters who will draw reluctant readers into the sphere of alien conspiracy and espionage . . . fast-paced and well-defined world will keep readers glued to the pages."

—SCHOOL LIBRARY JOURNAL

"Lewis is a veteran of the comic-book industry, and his plot is a domestic read-alike of Alex Rider."

—KIRKUS REVIEWS

"A fun read."

—PUBLISHERS WEEKLY

". . . Crackling plot twists, cliffhanger chapter endings, cyber attacks, alien invaders, and an undercurrent of teen romance."

—BOOKVIEWS BY ALAN CARUBA

Invasion

ALIENATION

A C.H.A.O.S. NOVEL

ALIENATION

A C.H.A.O.S. NOVEL

JON S. LEWIS

THOMAS NELSON
Since 1798

NASHVILLE DALLAS MEXICO CITY RIO DE JANEIRO

Published in Nashville, Tennessee, by Thomas Nelson. Thomas Nelson is a registered trademark of Thomas Nelson, Inc.

Scripture quotations are taken from The King James Version of the Bible.

Thomas Nelson, Inc., books may be purchased in bulk for educational, business, fund-raising, or sales promotional use. For information, please e-mail SpecialMarkets@ThomasNelson.com.

The author is represented by the literary agency of Alive Communications, Inc., 7680 Goddard Street, Suite 200, Colorado Springs, Colorado, 80920, www.alivecommunications.com.

ISBN 978-1-40168-556-0 (trade paper)

Library of Congress Cataloging-in-Publication Data

Lewis, Jon S.

  Alienation : a C.H.A.O.S. novel / Jon S. Lewis.
    p. cm. -- (A C.H.A.O.S. novel ; 2)
  Summary: Sixteen-year-old Colt McAllister, now in training at the secret Central Headquarters Against the Occult and Supernatural academy, joins in the battle against alien forces and discovers startling truths about himself, his friendship with Oz, and why he is being singled out from his fellow recruits.
  ISBN 978-1-59554-754-5 (hardcover)
  [1. Secret societies--Fiction. 2. Adventure and adventurers--Fiction. 3. Extraterrestrial beings--Fiction. 4. Supernatural--Fiction. 5. Conduct of life--Fiction. 6. Arizona--Fiction.] I. Title.
  PZ7.L5871Ali 2012
  [Fic]--dc22

2011036212

Printed in the United States of America

12 13 14 15 16 17 QG 6 5 4 3 2 1

For Kelly, Bailey, Olivia, and Lauren Lewis,
who love me even when I don't deserve it.

And for Lee Hough, who is fighting the good fight.

IN 1907, LORD FRANCIS BEEDLES LED A TEAM OF EXPLORERS TO THE GREEK ISLAND OF CRETE. THEY WERE LOOKING FOR THE LABYRINTH WHERE THESEUS SLEW THE MINOTAUR. WHAT THEY DISCOVERED WAS EVEN MORE REMARKABLE.

DEEP INSIDE A CAVE NEAR THE RUINS OF KNOSSOS WERE PICTOGRAPHS OF STRANGE CREATURES THAT LOOKED LIKE WALKING LIZARDS. IT WAS A CURIOUS FIND.

SO WAS THE GATEWAY, A DOOR THAT SOMEHOW LED THEM TO A STRANGE NEW WORLD . . .

A WORLD POPULATED BY THE VERY CREATURES THEY HAD FOUND ON THE WALLS.

YEARS LATER THERE WERE RUMORS THAT HITLER FOUND AN ENCLAVE OF THE LIZARD MEN, AND THAT HE ENLISTED TO FIGHT IN HIS ARMY.

IN RESPONSE, THE UNITED STATES FORMED THE CENTRAL HEADQUARTERS AGAINST THE OCCULT AND SUPERNATURAL.

CHAOS AGENTS LEARNED THAT THE LIZARD MEN WERE A RACE OF WARMONGERS KNOWN AS THE THULE.

OVER THE CENTURIES THEY HAD EXPANDED THEIR EMPIRE BY DESTROYING WORLD AFTER WORLD. NOW THAT THEIR OWN PLANET WAS DYING, THEY SOUGHT THE EARTH AS THEIR NEW HOME.

WHEN AMERICAN TROOPS LEARNED ABOUT THE PROPHECY, IT GAVE THEM AN IDEA . . .

DESPERATE TO END THE WAR, GIS INJECTED THEMSELVES WITH THE BLOOD FROM AN ALIEN CADAVER. THEY HOPED IT WOULD TURN AT LEAST ONE OF THEM INTO THE BETRAYER.

IT DIDN'T WORK. BUT THE UNITED STATES GOVERNMENT ADAPTED THE TEST AND SECRETLY INJECTED THOUSANDS OF MEN AND BOYS WITH A SERUM THAT CONTAINED ALIEN DNA.

IT TOOK MORE THAN FIFTY YEARS, BUT THEY FINALLY FOUND A MATCH.

AS THE THULE PREPARE TO INVADE, OUR LEADERS PRAY THAT COLT MCALISTER TRULY IS THE ONE . . . THAT HE IS THE BETRAYER.

:: **CHAPTER 1** ::

Colt McAlister burst from a bank of clouds with his arms pinned to his sides for maximum speed. The wind pounded his cheeks, sending waves across his skin as he clenched his jaw to keep from swallowing more insects. The aviator goggles kept his eyes from drying out, but he'd forgotten to wear his scarf. Or maybe he needed a mask. Either way, there was nothing worse than swallowing a moth, especially the big ones that got stuck in his throat.

The jet pack strapped to his back was an antique from the Second World War, and it shook his body from his toes to his teeth, but it didn't matter. The thrill of flying was like nothing else. Roller coasters. Bungee jumping. Cliff diving. Even surfing. None of it compared to roaring through the sky without a safety net.

The sun peeked out from behind the Superstition Mountains, casting the morning in a strange haze as an October wind blew across the desert. Colt could see his breath whenever he exhaled, but he ignored the cold and arched his shoulders, throwing his head back as he shot straight up. Lost in the moment, Colt let the world and all its worries fade away. Up there, problems had a way of disappearing. There were no thoughts of alien invasions, secret mind-control programs, or his parents, who had been murdered just a few short weeks ago.

At times he missed them so intensely that the simple act of breathing became impossible. He would go to his room, turn off the lights, and crawl into bed, wishing he could be with them again—even if it meant dying. In those empty moments, life felt meaningless. Hopeless.

"I'm just about set up." The voice that crackled through his earpiece belonged to Danielle Salazar, who was on the ground setting up the obstacle course. She was a video game expert, computer hacker, and one of Colt's best friends. They were born days apart, and even though they weren't related by blood, he thought of her as the sister he never had.

People who didn't know them just figured they were dating. After all, they didn't look anything like siblings. His mop of hair was so blond it looked white in the summer, and his eyes were the kind of blue that made people think he wore colored contacts. Everything about Danielle was dark. Her hair. Eyes. Skin. Colt could admit that she was beautiful, but date her? Not in this lifetime.

"I'll be right there." He pulled up and hovered in place, distracted by a pair of hawks flying in circles. Their dance was beautiful, effortless, and he could have watched them for hours, but the older model jet packs didn't have reliable fuel gauges. It read that he had less than seven minutes remaining, which was enough time to run the obstacle course at least once, but there was no way to know for sure. Still, he needed the practice. Yesterday's effort had been a disaster.

He turned and headed back to the ground where Danielle was

waiting near his grandpa's 1946 Chevy pickup with the chrome grill and whitewall tires. The 1974 Toyota Land Cruiser that his parents bought for his sixteenth birthday was in storage back in San Diego.

The exhaust from his jet pack sent a swirl of dust and sand rolling across the desert as he touched down. Landing was still awkward, and he stumbled before he regained his footing, but at least he didn't roll his ankle or run into a cactus.

"All right," Danielle said. She was wearing a thick jacket wreathed in some kind of fake fur, and vapors from the cold escaped from between her lips as she entered a sequence of commands into her tablet computer. "The targets are all set up, so as soon as Oz gets here—if he gets here—we can start."

Oz Romero was perpetually late. It didn't matter if he was going to a class, doctor's appointment, church, or movie. Timeliness and Oz simply didn't mix. Most of the time it didn't matter, but this morning Colt had forced himself out of bed at five thirty. If he had to be on time, he expected the same from Oz.

Colt flipped his goggles up over his helmet as he watched the gravel road. He wanted to give Oz the benefit of the doubt. Maybe he was having engine trouble, or he'd stopped to help someone change a flat tire. Or maybe he was just late, like always. "Where is he?"

"He won't answer his phone, which means he's probably still asleep."

"What do you want to do?"

"I don't know," Danielle said. "I mean, we're out here, and everything is set up. You might as well run the course. If he doesn't show up by the time you have to refuel, we can head back."

She was about to climb into the cab and sit next to the heater when a black Jeep crested a hill. Dust plumed and oversized tires crunched across the desert floor, leaving a massive trail in the Jeep's wake. At the last possible moment, Oz pulled off the road and parked between a saguaro cactus and Grandpa's pickup.

"You're late," Danielle said with a hand on her hip.

Oz shrugged and cut the engine before he gulped down the last of a protein shake and wiped his mouth with the back of his sleeve. "Sorry." It wasn't much of an apology. Usually he would have made some outlandish excuse and then laughed it off.

He hopped out of the Jeep, his eyes distant. He looked tired, or was it depressed? Either way, it wasn't normal. Oz was typically upbeat, whether the occasion called for it or not.

"What's wrong? Were you up all night hunting zombies again?" Colt asked, referring to Zombie Extermination Squad, a video game that the three of them played together more often than they cared to admit.

Oz looked at him and frowned, as though trying to gauge if he was serious. "You heard about the incident, right?"

Colt hadn't, but that wasn't unusual. Oz had access to information the rest of the world didn't know existed. His dad was the director of an organization called CHAOS—Central Headquarters Against the Occult and Supernatural. They were a bit like the CIA or the FBI, but instead of going after drug cartels or spying on the Russians, they protected the world from nightmares like bioengineered monsters, alien life forms, and sparkling vampires.

"Can you give us a hint?" Colt asked. The way things had been going lately, he half expected Oz to tell him that Godzilla had been spotted off the shores of Tokyo.

"Turn on the radio and you'll see." Oz slipped into a jumpsuit that he had pulled out of his duffel bag. It didn't look like it was going to fit his six-foot-four frame or his enormous shoulders, but he managed to squeeze in and zip it up before he slipped on a pair of size fifteen boots.

Danielle turned the key in the ignition of the pickup, and static blasted through the speakers as she tried to find a news station.

". . . thousands are seeking refuge, shutting down roads and freeways leading from Cedar Rapids and surrounding communities despite the combined efforts of local law enforcement and the National Guard. Already airports in Des Moines, Minneapolis, Chicago, and Kansas City have been overrun with people looking to get as far away from the reactor core as possible."

"Reactor core?" Colt asked. "What happened?"

"They're telling everyone that there was a leak at a nuclear power plant, but that's just a cover," Oz said.

"For what?" Danielle asked. After all, a meltdown at a reactor could be catastrophic, but if that was just a story, the truth had to be devastating.

"They think someone released a virus."

"What, like the bird flu or something?" Colt asked.

Oz shook his head. "Worse. And it's spreading fast."

:: CHAPTER 2 ::

Oz quickly told them that the first known case of the virus had been documented two weeks prior in a remote village outside of Bangkok. An old woman contracted a fever, and by nightfall her skin was covered in boils. Breathing became increasingly difficult, and within forty-eight hours she was dead. Three others got sick before government authorities were notified, and once that happened the village was quarantined. If the rumors were true, at least a dozen infected people had been shot and their bodies burned.

Without a corpse there was no way to run an autopsy, but days later a similar case surfaced in Veracruz, a port city on the Gulf of Mexico. Seven employees at a nuclear facility ended up with the same boils, and they were dead inside two days. A third instance occurred on a Navajo reservation near Page, Arizona. And now, just that morning, more than twenty people were infected just outside of Cedar Rapids. Most of them worked at the Duane Arnold Energy Center, the only nuclear power plant in Iowa.

Military officials had set up checkpoints to test everyone before they were allowed to leave the contaminated zone. The infected were led away by men in hazmat suits as armed soldiers wearing gas masks stood by to ensure there were no riots.

"My dad thinks it's a biological attack," Oz said. "I guess it makes sense. We shut down the gateways before the Thule could send their warships through, so now they have to try something more creative if they want to wipe us out."

"But there's a cure, right?" Colt said.

"Not exactly, but they're working on it."

"So what happens when the virus hits a major city like New York or Los Angeles?"

Oz put his enormous hand on Colt's shoulder. "You better pray that it doesn't," he said. "Because once that happens, we won't be able to contain it."

As he watched Oz strap on his jet pack, Colt was stricken by a terrible thought. He and Oz were supposed to transfer to the CHAOS Military Academy in a few days, but now it seemed meaningless. Fighting aliens was one thing, but how was humanity supposed to wage war against a virus that killed people within forty-eight hours? It's not like you could shoot it or anything. Besides, even if someone found a cure, there was no way pharmaceutical companies could manufacture enough of the antidote for everyone—at least not soon enough.

"Relax," Oz said, as though reading Colt's mind. "The good guys always win. Besides, we have bigger things to worry about."

"Like what?"

"Making sure you actually finish the obstacle course." Oz smiled, and for a fleeting moment everything felt almost normal.

Almost, because Colt knew that "normal" was never going to describe his life again. Recently he had learned that a group of influential politicians and military personnel wanted to remove

Oz's dad as the director of CHAOS. And ridiculous as it sounded, Colt was on the short list of people they were looking at to replace him, despite the fact that he was only sixteen. There was nothing normal about it. More than anything, he just hoped that it didn't ruin his relationship with Oz.

Since they weren't going to finish the semester at Chandler High School, the boys had been excused from class for the past three weeks. But instead of sitting around and watching television or playing video games, they spent their time training for the academy. That meant stretching, running, lifting weights, target practice, and a lot of sparring. Oz had taught Colt bits of Krav Maga, Brazilian Jiu-Jitsu, boxing, and even some wrestling techniques.

He had a shooting range at his house, and Colt was making good progress, considering he had never held a firearm before. Hitting a stationary target with both feet on the ground was hard enough; trying to shoot it while wearing a jet pack and going over eighty miles per hour through the air was just short of impossible.

Tuesday was their second day running the obstacle course. Colt had been humiliated during the first go-round, and he was determined to perform better. He checked his gauges and the connections on his fuel tank, and a few moments later he was rocketing through the clouds with Oz at his side.

Colt looked like a throwback to the 1940s in his olive green fatigues, leather bomber jacket, and oversized aviator goggles. None of his gear offered much in the way of protection, but he thought the flight suits were too restrictive. Oz, on the other hand, looked like he had just stepped out of the future. His helmet covered his entire face, making him look more machine than man, and the armored jumpsuit resembled a military-grade motorcross uniform. It was made out of fibers that were supposedly bullet-resistant, like Kevlar, only stronger.

"Who's going first?" Danielle asked, her voice crackling through the comlink as she watched them from below.

"That would be me!" The exhaust from Oz's rocket burned bright as he disappeared into a bank of clouds.

Danielle had set up ten targets at random intervals across the desert floor. Once activated, the metal discs projected holograms that could look like anything. Today she had programmed ten six-armed aliens called Thule, each of them snarling, their lips curled to reveal crooked teeth.

"Watch and learn, McAlister." Oz dived and Danielle started her stopwatch.

From where Colt watched, it looked like Oz was going to crash before he leveled at about thirty feet and pulled out a pistol that hung at his hip. The Tesla 6000 Electrostatic Repulsor had been retrofitted as a training weapon, so it shot light rays instead of energy blasts.

Oz had the uncanny knack of making the impossible look mundane, and he hit the first three targets in eighteen seconds without so much as slowing down. He hit a fourth that was partially hidden behind a cactus, and a fifth that was gnashing its teeth on a rocky embankment.

"How many did you hit yesterday?" Oz asked as he spun the repulsor on his finger.

Before Colt could answer, Danielle pulled the statistics up on her tablet computer. "He ran the course five times and hit seven targets, which means his accuracy rating is at just over 14 percent."

"Thanks," Colt said.

"Don't mention it."

Distracted, Oz flew too close to the sixth hologram. It reached out, and at the last possible moment Oz swiveled his hips, avoiding contact that would have led to a penalty. Then, as though it was as natural as walking, he rolled over so that he was lying on his back, raised the repulsor, and shot. Direct hit. The hologram flickered and disappeared. The last four holograms fell in succession, giving Oz another perfect score.

"Your turn."

:: CHAPTER 3 ::

Colt chewed on the inside of his cheek as he took aim at the first hologram. The attention to detail was incredible, from the light glinting off the Thule's eyes to the way its scaled chest heaved with every breath. If he hadn't known better, he would have sworn that it was real.

"You got this," Oz said. He was back on the ground, standing next to Danielle. "Remember, aim . . . exhale . . . and then pull the trigger. It's as easy as that."

The first target was about fifty feet away, and Colt was closing fast. He exhaled. Ten meters. Colt could almost smell the alien's rancid breath as he closed his eyes and pulled the trigger.

Somehow the beam of light hit the creature's shoulder. It wasn't a kill shot, but the alien roared as it grabbed the imaginary wound. Colt couldn't help but smile as the image flickered before it disappeared. It was the first time he'd ever hit the initial target.

There was no time to celebrate. The second target beat its chest with two hands while the other four flexed sharp claws, waiting to tear him apart. Colt veered toward the hologram as an angry wind buffeted against him, but he hardly noticed. Gritting his teeth, he raised the Tesla Repulsor and steadied his wrist, just as Oz had done. The creature threw its head back, and Colt aimed for its throat. He took a slow breath, exhaled, and squeezed the trigger.

And missed. The alien didn't flicker, flash, or disappear.

Colt raised his arms to cover his face, and his jacket took the brunt of the punishment. He blinked, and when he opened his eyes all he could see was the parched ground. It was ten meters away, and it was closing fast.

He raised his head and arched his back, extending his arms like wings as he attempted to rise. Something hissed behind his ear. Had the tank been punctured? Maybe one of the hoses was dislodged. Colt thought that he could smell fuel, but maybe it was the exhaust.

The ground was closer now. He could reach out and touch it if he had half a mind, but he strained his neck and threw his shoulders back, hoping that would be enough. The desert grime was thick on his tongue, gritty and raw. Strange shapes loomed ahead. It was a wall of cactus, twisted and bent.

His left hand scraped the ground, bouncing as it skimmed the surface like a stone skipping across a pond. His fist hit a rock and the Tesla Repulsor fell from his hand. The gun clanked, breaking into countless pieces as it bounced away. He turned his head for the briefest moment to see where it landed, but the movement drove his shoulder into the ground.

"Pull up!" Oz shouted through the comlink.

Pain shot through Colt's shoulder and up into his neck. Jaw clenched and eyes filled with tears, he rolled to his right, trying to correct his haphazard path. The tank sputtered, spitting out a trail of smoke as it backfired.

"Not now," Colt said, straining through gritted teeth as he fought to keep from crashing. It felt like the tendons in his neck were going to snap, but his body rose even as the fuel tank lost pressure.

The jet pack shook, threatening to break free from the straps that held it in place, and Colt felt the tremors through his body. His teeth chattered and his vision blurred as he pulled away from the desert floor and up into the early morning haze.

"Are you trying to give me a heart attack?" Danielle asked.

Colt couldn't answer. His heart pounded as he tilted to the right, his shoulder dipping as he entered into a barrel roll. Like a corkscrew, he shot straight up, avoiding the cactus as a great plume of smoke trailed in his wake. It felt like he was coming up for air after holding his breath under water for too long. Relief washed over him, and he closed his eyes for a brief moment to drink it in. The world was quiet. Calm. Far below, a tumbleweed rolled across the desert, bouncing in the wind before it caught on a shrub.

The jet pack sputtered, a reminder that he needed to land before his fuel supply ran out. He didn't know the odds of surviving a thousand-foot fall, but he figured they weren't in his favor. Just then he heard a strange buzzing sound. It was faint at first, like the hum of an oscillating fan, but it was growing louder.

"Do you hear that?" he asked, tilting his head like a dog listening to a distant noise.

"Hear what?" Oz asked.

"I'm not sure." Colt tapped on the tiny speaker lodged in his ear, wondering if it was feedback. "It's like a hum, or—"

A massive silhouette rose from the mountains, wings beating and teeth gnashing as it flew toward him.

:: CHAPTER 4 ::

P lease tell me that's another hologram," Colt said as the creature closed in. It was the size of a small bus, with a body that
looked something like a wasp, though it was covered in a
spiny exoskeleton. Two sets of enormous wings kept it aloft, beating rapidly as six spiked legs hung limp below its belly.

"If it is, it's not one of mine," Danielle said from below. "I don't
know how to make them fly yet."

"It's called an armored viper wasp," Oz said. "And trust me, it's
real. Let's just hope there isn't a hive nearby."

"A hive?"

The wasp looked like it could bring down an elephant if it had
half a mind, but a swarm of those things? There wasn't enough
bug spray on the planet to deal with that kind of infestation. Its
teeth looked like gardening shears, and they stuck out from its
mouth in haphazard directions, as though their placement was
completely random yet altogether deadly.

"Now would be a good time to get out of there," Oz said, but
Colt couldn't move. The surrounding mountains started to feel
like walls, and the vast desert no bigger than a closet.

"Come on, McAlister!" Oz said. "What are you doing?"

Colt didn't respond, even though it was close enough that he could see scars etched into its armored hide. Why couldn't he move?

"Look, I want you to get in the truck and drive as far away as you can," Colt heard Oz say through the comlink. "We'll be right behind you. I promise."

"But . . ." Danielle's voice was hesitant.

"Don't be a hero," Oz said. "Just go!"

The viper wasp lashed out with deceptive speed, and Colt had the good sense to duck. He felt a rush of air sweep over his head as the creature screeched like an orchestra of first-year violin students.

Far below, Dani jumped into the cab of the truck. The engine revved and tires spun, spitting dirt and rock as it fishtailed and headed back toward the freeway.

"Heads up!" Oz said. There was silence, followed by the sound of rushing air, like a vacuum cleaner, only amplified a thousand-fold. A jagged beam of light slammed into the mindless creature, scorching its exoskeleton. The burning smell was nauseating, and Colt had to fight to keep from throwing up.

The viper wasp kicked its legs as it tumbled backward through the morning sky, screaming as its wings pounded against the wind. Viscous matter oozed from the wound, and for a moment Colt almost felt sorry for it. Almost.

He took advantage of the diversion and dived. Sparks flew and smoke streamed as one of the engines on his jet pack died. He closed his eyes as he continued to fall, wondering if a single engine was enough to carry him. It would be so easy to give up. No more pain. No more heartache. He imagined his parents standing there, arms wide, waiting to embrace him.

But it wasn't his time.

Colt looked over his shoulder, where the beast was clacking its jaws open and shut. Despite the wound, its wings fluttered so fast they were a blur, and it was gaining ground. Colt fought to maintain balance. With only one working rocket, flight was awkward. It felt like he was weighed down on one side.

"Now what?" he asked.

"I have an idea, but it's going to be risky," Oz said. "Do you remember that cartoon where the mouse tricks the cat into swallowing a stick of dynamite?"

"Yeah, why?"

"Well, I don't have any dynamite, but there's a belt filled with concussion grenades in the backseat of the Jeep. Think you can get that thing to eat a couple of them?"

"You're serious?"

"It's all I've got."

It was an insane plan, but Colt was desperate. He dived toward the Jeep as Oz grabbed the belt. In one swift motion Oz flicked his wrist and tossed it into the air just as Colt's second engine sputtered and cut out. He hit the ignition switch a few times, but it didn't so much as spark, let alone turn over. Then, after another try, it sparked back to life.

He shot straight up and grabbed the belt. Momentum took him past the confused wasp as he fastened the belt around his waist with nervous fingers. In rapid succession he fished out three concussion grenades, each activated in mere seconds.

The viper wasp gave chase, unwilling to let its prey escape. That's exactly what Colt was counting on. He hovered in place, waiting for the creature to get within range. Wind rushed as wings pounded, and he let the first grenade fall. It rolled off his fingers and hit the wasp in the teeth before it bounced off.

Colt's eyes shot wide.

The beast howled, jaws open wide as it bore down on him. Colt looked down its throat and wondered if this was how Jonah felt before the whale swallowed him whole.

"That was part of the plan, right?" he heard Oz ask.

Colt looked down at the two flashing grenades in his hand, and then at the viper wasp. It gave a screech, and he tossed them down its wide gullet. The cries of the beast stopped as it pulled up, looking confused.

Moments later explosions reverberated through the desert, and the viper wasp was blown into chunks of disgusting goop. Guts splattered like gelatinous rain, covering rocks, cacti, and shrubs.

"You're paying to wash my Jeep," Oz said.

:: CHAPTER 5 ::

It had been years since anyone had called Santiago Romero by his given name. The director of CHAOS was known simply as Lobo, the Spanish word for wolf. There were many stories as to how he got the name, but one thing was certain—it fit. The man was cunning, strong, and ruthless.

It was Tuesday morning, and he sat alone in the lobby of the Mandarin Oriental Hotel, just a few blocks away from the White House. In less than a week his son, Oz, would arrive to attend the CHAOS Military Academy just outside of Alexandria. He was excited and a bit nervous, as any father would be considering what was at stake. Oz had spent his entire life preparing to become a CHAOS agent, and this was his moment to shine.

As the director, Lobo typically spent his days in meetings or seated at his desk, but he still carried a Sig Sauer P226 with a twenty-round magazine beneath his suit coat. He had another forty rounds hidden in the leather satchel near his foot. It was all a precaution—or perhaps it was habit. Either way, he felt better knowing that the weapon was near.

There were also five armed agents in and around the hotel,

including a man posing as a bell captain who had a Benelli M4 Super 90 shotgun hidden behind the bell stand. The elevator repairman had an HK MP5 submachine gun in his tool kit and an MK23 .45 caliber handgun in a holster hidden beneath his coveralls. Then there was the agent stationed in a tree just outside the bay window, armed with an M14 sniper rifle. He was wearing a ghillie suit, heavily camouflaged clothes that were designed to look like foliage, and even though Lobo knew he was out there, he couldn't see him.

Given the nature of this meeting, the precaution felt prudent. After all, Heinrich Krone was not only an assassin of the highest order, he was also one of the Thule.

Lobo looked at his watch and saw that it was five minutes to eight. He sipped a cup of English breakfast tea with just a touch of honey as he read the *Washington Post*. The lead story was about the reactor leak in Iowa. Over a hundred thousand residents had been tested for radiation poisoning, with fifty-six testing positive. According to the article, they had been transferred to a nearby hospital, but Lobo knew the truth. They had contracted the mysterious virus that appeared out of nowhere, and they were all going to die.

A special investigation unit stationed at a CHAOS facility in Chicago had been sent to collect samples. The strain had mutated, but they were convinced it was the same virus found in Thailand, Mexico, and Arizona. What they didn't know was where it had come from or how it got there. Investigators pored over travel logs from every major airline, bus, and railway that served the cities in question, but there was no passenger overlap. They even searched the homes and businesses of the infected, but they couldn't find a point of origin. It didn't make sense.

A CHAOS agent disguised as a member of the hotel waitstaff stopped by to freshen Lobo's teapot. He offered his thanks and handed her a twenty-dollar bill, which she stuffed into her apron next to her Sig Sauer P230. She nodded and headed back to the kitchen with a wide smile.

Lobo had been staying at the Mandarin on and off for almost two weeks. His wife was back in Arizona with their son, and he was surprising her with some renovations at their Virginia countryside estate. With construction crews traipsing about, staying at the hotel was easier. Besides, the room service was amazing, maids cleaned his suite every morning, and the hotel was close enough to the office that it cut nearly thirty minutes off his commute.

As he waited for his appointment to arrive, his dark eyes roved the lobby floor, looking for anything unusual. Outside of the hotel staff and his undercover agents, there wasn't much activity. A woman stood at the front desk with ten pieces of luggage, wondering if she could check in early. An older couple were on their way out for a morning walk, and a man with a pronounced bald spot and a hawkish nose was asking the concierge for directions to an office complex where he was already late for a client meeting.

The front door slid open, and a brisk wind blew through the lobby. A thin man wearing a long coat walked inside. He wore a driving cap and leather gloves, but instead of luggage he was carrying a briefcase. It was difficult to gauge his age, though he looked to be somewhere in his late twenties or maybe early thirties.

"Krone?" Lobo asked as the man approached. Even though he was born in San Antonio, Lobo still had an accent. His parents were from the city of Reynosa in Tamualipas, Mexico, and he didn't speak English until he was six years old.

Krone nodded. As a shapeshifter, the man could have taken just about any form he desired, and he did so regularly. It made him a unique asset in the global espionage and intelligence community, though at the moment he didn't look much like an assassin—or at least the kind of assassin you might find in a Hollywood movie. He was not heavily muscled, his head wasn't shaved, and there were no visible tattoos. In fact, he was impeccably groomed, from his short-cropped hair to his manicured nails. His suit was clearly custom tailored, and Lobo assumed that his jacket was as well. The scarf was no doubt cashmere, and his wing-tipped shoes had been recently shined.

"Please, take a seat." Lobo nodded to an empty couch across from where he was sitting.

Krone set his briefcase down, took off his gloves, and removed his coat, which he folded neatly before he laid it across the arm of the couch. As he sat, his eyes fell to the newspaper and then to Lobo, who watched him intently.

"A pity what happened in Iowa, wouldn't you agree?" Lobo asked.

The man nodded. "Yes, it was. Hopefully we won't have another Chernobyl on our hands."

"Let's hope not." Lobo smiled, though the expression held little kindness. Krone no doubt knew that there was no reactor leak, but that wasn't important—at least for the moment.

"Tea?" Lobo asked, but the man held up his hand.

"No, thank you."

Lobo reached down and unfastened the latch on his satchel to pull out a manila folder, which he slid across the coffee table.

"My assignment, I presume?" Krone took the folder and opened it to find the photograph of an older man who looked to be in his sixties or seventies. He was handsome and tanned, probably from spending too much time on the golf course. His teeth were perfect, as was his silver hair, and there was a pin of the Stars and Stripes fastened to his lapel.

Krone stared at the image as though memorizing every detail, then he closed the folder and handed it back to Lobo. "It won't be easy, you know," he said, as his eyes fell on a gardener pruning a bush just outside the window. It was another one of Lobo's agents, and it was clear that Krone had spotted him. "Eliminating Senator Bishop is going to draw attention. After all, your feud has been rather public. And it's going to look like sour grapes—you know, with him leading the charge to cut your funding until you're replaced."

"I understand the ramifications, but at this point we don't have a choice." Lobo took a sip of his tea. "If the senator and his cronies had their way, I'd be rotting in a cell next to Aldrich Koenig right now. They think I've turned CHAOS into my own private army, and they're scared—not that I can blame them. In their minds, my methods are . . . well, I suppose they would consider them aggressive. Brutal. Perhaps they are, but they're also effective. The odds of this planet surviving an attack from your people are already infinitesimal—without me, they're nonexistent."

"So they've left you with no choice, is that it?"

Lobo regarded the assassin, sensing that he was being mocked. "You're going to make the senator's demise look like an accident. Or better yet, like a natural death." Lobo lowered his voice. "The man turned seventy years old last month, and he's already had one open-heart surgery. I'm sure you'll find a creative solution to ensure the least amount of scrutiny."

"Perhaps I'll have that cup of tea after all." Krone reached for the pot of steaming water and poured some into a cup before adding a teabag and a bit of cream. "You know, it's rather odd," he said, voice calm, face devoid of emotion. "I mean, here we've worked together for, what is it now . . . nearly a decade? Yet we've never had the pleasure of meeting before today. If you don't mind my asking, why now?"

Lobo sat at the edge of the couch, leaning forward. His forearms rested on his knees and his fingers were interlocked as he looked directly at Krone. "I need to know that I can trust you," he said. "And the only way to know if you can trust a man is to look him in the eyes."

"I see," Krone said, unflinching under the scrutiny. "Have I given you a reason to question my loyalty?"

"I've never been the trusting sort," Lobo said. "It's not terribly prudent in our line of work, as I'm sure you would agree."

Krone bowed his head, acknowledging the truth of the statement.

"I'll be frank," Lobo said. "There is an entire planet filled with monsters like you, and they're all chomping at the bit to turn Earth into their new home. It's my job to make sure that doesn't happen, and that alone is enough for me to doubt your loyalties."

"So I'm a monster, am I?" Krone asked, looking relaxed as he sipped his tea. Lobo started to clarify his point, but Krone raised his hand to cut him off. "I understand what you're saying, and it's a perfectly fair point."

"So why should I trust you?"

"You shouldn't."

Lobo narrowed his eyes.

"Look, I could give you a litany of reasons why I won't betray our pact," Krone said. "I could start with the fact that I was born here on Earth and have very little love for my home world. I could tell you that you've paid me handsomely over the years, affording me a lifestyle I might never have known. But we both know none of that matters."

He set his cup back on the saucer. "There are other important people besides Senator Bishop who would like to see you replaced. Who's to say I won't align myself with them should your downfall become imminent? Or if they simply offer more money?"

"And your response?"

"Here's the thing," Krone said after a lengthy pause. "You need me, and I always deliver. Trust has nothing to do with it. Besides, my record stands for itself. Once I accept a contract, I don't break it."

Lobo sat with jaw clenched and brows furrowed. With a single word, his agents could eliminate Krone if it came to that, but the assassin was right. Trust was impossible. Even foolish. "Then I take it you'll accept the job under our current terms?"

"I'm afraid not," Krone said. "I'll need double the usual number, half wired to my account within the hour and the other half payable once the job is complete."

"Then it needs to happen tonight," Lobo said. "Senator Bishop is set to speak at a fund-raiser for a congressional candidate in Tucson. Your flight leaves in an hour."

:: CHAPTER 6 ::

Lobo arranged for a private jet to fly Krone from Ronald Reagan Washington National Airport to Tucson, where a driver took him to the Ventana Canyon Resort. Though it was late October, the sun was shining in the vast blue sky. It was perfect weather for golf, and Senator Bishop was about to tee off on the third hole of the Mountain Course. He was there with Jeff Wilson, the Republican nominee for the 8th Congressional District, along with a Secret Service agent and two influential donors who had organized the thousand-dollar-a-plate fundraiser for Wilson's campaign.

The Republicans hoped to regain control of the United States Congress, and this was one of the races they were banking on to get their majority. Polls showed that Wilson trailed the Democratic incumbent, Alicia Alvarez, by six points. The hope was that an endorsement from Senator Bishop—not to mention the contributions from that evening—would be enough to push Wilson past Alvarez.

Krone tipped the driver handsomely and walked into the lobby, which was filled with middle-aged men in golf shirts and khaki pants, as well as beautiful women wearing designer clothes and expensive jewelry. It was no doubt a gathering of Tucson's elite—doctors, lawyers, and entrepreneurs, as well as a television anchor whom Krone recognized from one of the twenty-four-hour cable news stations.

"So much for the impartiality of the press," he said under his breath.

Krone thought about posing as one of the housekeepers, or even as a waiter delivering room service, but with the Secret Service agents hovering around the senator's room, there were too many eyes. Better, he thought, to wait for the dinner, where things could be more discreet.

He spent the rest of the afternoon at the bar, where he watched television and enjoyed a grilled portabella mushroom sandwich with avocados and sprouts. The news was focused on the reactor leak in Iowa. All across the Midwest, churches, homeless shelters, and even a chain of health clubs had opened their doors to take in displaced families.

As the afternoon lingered, the bar started to empty. People went back to their rooms to get ready for dinner, leaving Krone alone with the bartender. He looked down at his watch. The wait-staff was set to meet in the Grand Ballroom in ten minutes, so he finished off his bottle of sparkling water and paid for his tab in cash.

As Krone walked across the grounds back toward the main building, he pulled out his phone and opened an image of the employee he was going to impersonate. Israel Sandoval was a twenty-three-year-old college graduate who had recently been accepted to the University of Arizona medical school. He was handsome, like a Latin pop star, but more important he had just moved to town. That meant he hadn't been on the job long enough for anyone to grow accustomed to the nuances of his inflection or body movement.

That afternoon the real Israel received a call from his supervisor. According to the Secret Service, employees who hadn't been at the resort for at least three months weren't allowed to work the event. But the person on the other end of the call wasn't his supervisor at all. It was Krone.

Krone walked through a service door and into a winding labyrinth of hallways. His skin started to bubble, and for a moment it looked like it was melting. Bone cracked and cartilage shifted, his blue eyes faded to brown, and his hair grew longer. In the blink of an eye, Krone became a living replica of Israel Sandoval. And short of a blood test, no one other than his mother would know the difference.

He removed his watch, cuff links, jacket, and tie, then placed them all in his briefcase, which he hid behind a bin of white tablecloths. Then he rolled up his sleeves and walked into the employee locker room.

A heavyset man in his early twenties greeted him as though they knew each other. He had a mass of red hair and he was trying to fasten a cummerbund around the girth of his stomach. He wasn't having much luck. Krone forced a smile as he nodded and waved. It was best to avoid talking whenever possible. Mimicking other voices had always been the most difficult part of the job, and even though he had listened to tapes of Israel talking during his flight, Krone wasn't sure he could pull it off on such short notice.

He walked over to the rack of uniforms hanging across the back wall and found the one with Israel's name pinned to the

jacket. He changed into a tuxedo with a black bow tie and matching cummerbund and listened to the banquet manager, who was
flanked by two Secret Service agents.

"Can you believe this?"

Krone turned to see the man with the red hair standing next
to him, smiling.

"I mean, Senator Bishop is the first presidential candidate I
ever voted for. Do you think they'll fire me if I try and get a picture with him?"

:: CHAPTER 7 ::

It didn't take long for the tables in the dining hall to fill up. Krone was assigned to a section in the back of the room that included a table for local media, but somehow the guy with the red hair, whose name was Harry, was up front serving Senator Bishop's table.

Once everyone was seated, salads were served and the program began. The emcee for the evening welcomed the guests and thanked them for their generous contributions before saying a few words about Jeff Wilson.

"How's it going over there?" Krone asked as Harry walked over to the bar with a tray of empty glassware.

"Terrible." Harry took a stack of napkins and dabbed at the perspiration that beaded on his forehead.

"Is he a jerk or something?"

"No, nothing like that," Harry said as he tossed the napkins into the trash.

"Then what's wrong?"

"I kind of spilled a pitcher of water on his wife."

Krone started to laugh.

"It's not funny," Harry said. "I'm going to get fired."

"Why don't you let me bring them another round of drinks? That way you can compose yourself before you head back over."

"I don't know . . ." Harry's voice trailed off as he looked back at the senator's table. "What if the Secret Service guys think I'm up to something?"

"After the stunt you just pulled, I'm pretty sure your name is already on a terrorist watch list." Krone smiled, trying to put Harry at ease.

"Okay, but just this round. I want to go put on more deodorant and get a new shirt. I'm sweating like a pig."

With Harry out of sight and the bartender distracted with another order, Krone reached into his jacket pocket to pull out a vial filled with a clear liquid called tetrodotoxin. The lethal neurotoxin is found in the liver of puffer fish, and there is no known antidote. He removed the lid with his thumb and poured the contents into Senator Bishop's vodka martini, which he quickly stirred before adding two olives.

Krone carried the tray of drinks on his fingertips like a seasoned professional, weaving through the tables. He was about to serve the senator's wife when one of the Secret Service agents grabbed him by the wrist.

"Who are you?" He was short, but he had broad shoulders and a thick neck, not to mention an FN Five-Seven semiautomatic pistol that he carried under his jacket.

"Harry asked me to deliver these," Krone said. "He's kind of flustered after what happened. I'm just helping him out."

"If you're going to pat him down, hurry up," Senator Bishop said from his seat at the table. "But let the man serve the drinks, Rusty."

The Secret Service agent bit the inside of his cheek as he looked from Krone to the drinks and then to the senator. Krone could tell that he was considering breaking protocol. With a sigh, Rusty waved him on.

"There's a good man," Senator Bishop said as he took a last bite of his salad.

"We're terribly sorry about the mishap," Krone said. "If there's anything we can do—"

"You're halfway there." The senator accepted the martini. "Now if you can make sure that everyone stays awake during my speech, we'll call it even." Everyone at the table laughed as Krone watched the senator take a sip of his drink.

A few minutes later Harry was back in a fresh shirt, smelling like a mixture of aerosol deodorant and drugstore aftershave. "How did it go?"

"Everything is going according to plan." Krone patted Harry on the back. "But you might want to see if Senator Bishop wants another martini. I think he already finished the last one."

Harry brought the senator another martini, returning a few minutes later with the dirty glass that held the evidence of the neurotoxin. Krone watched as it was placed on a tray before it was brought back to the kitchen.

The rest of the servers started to clear the dinner plates as the lights dimmed and the emcee returned to the stage. "So that's what a thousand-dollar filet mignon tastes like," he said, earning perfunctory laughter as he patted his stomach and smacked his lips. "Well, as long as it helps us regain Congress, it was well worth it!"

That time the crowd erupted, and the emcee basked in their applause before he raised his hands to quiet everyone down. "Now, without further ado, it is my distinguished honor to introduce the esteemed five-term senator from this great state of Arizona, the honorable Samuel Bishop."

The crowd rose in thunderous applause, and Krone watched as the senator wiped his mouth and then his brow before steadying himself against the table. His wife leaned over, concern on her face, but he patted her hand and smiled before he stood. The ovation continued as he walked to the stage, where he shook hands with the emcee. His face was pale, his brow covered in sweat as he turned to wave to the audience. Then he fell, unconscious.

A collective gasp rose from the audience as the emcee knelt next to him, confused. Secret Service agents rushed to the stage, and Krone slipped out the door and into the service corridor. His face morphed back to the way it had looked when he first arrived as he removed his tuxedo jacket and dumped it in the trash. He grabbed his briefcase and pulled out his phone to send a simple text.

It's done.

Moments later his phone beeped with a return message. It was the address of a home in Chandler, Arizona, along with a picture of a teenaged boy with blond hair that hung over his blue eyes.

:: CHAPTER 8 ::

A couple months ago life had been perfect. Colt had been living in San Diego, surfing and hanging out with his friends. Aliens and monsters were nothing more than fictional creatures, and if there was such a thing as a federal curfew, nobody enforced it. His family lived in a big house near the beach, his parents were alive and together, and they actually showed interest in his life.

The past felt like it belonged to someone else, something he could have read about or watched on television. It was too perfect, too pristine. And it was gone. His parents had been murdered, he'd moved to Arizona to live with his grandfather, and those aliens and monsters? It turned out they were real.

Law enforcement across the globe had been overrun with calls from people who had seen strange creatures from myth and legend, and now policemen patrolled the streets in riot gear carrying automatic weapons. Everyone under the age of eighteen had to be inside by ten o'clock, and in less than a week Colt was moving again—this time to a top secret military school in Virginia where they were going to train him to save the world.

The debate was finally over. There were at least eleven other planets that supported complex life forms, and for all Colt knew there could be thousands more. One of those life forms—a race of six-armed walking reptiles called the Thule—had picked Earth to be their next home, and they weren't interested in sharing it with the current residents.

It was just past nine o'clock on Tuesday night when Colt walked through the kitchen door and threw his keys on the countertop. He'd spent the last few hours at the shooting range with Oz, working on his marksmanship with a Jericho 941 semiautomatic pistol and a Dragunov SVD sniper rifle. It was a lot easier than flying through the air at eighty miles per hour and trying to hit holograms with a laser gun, but it would be years until he was as good as Oz.

He opened the refrigerator and pulled out a bucket of leftover chicken, but he didn't bother warming it up or even sitting down at the table. The television was on in the living room, tuned in to one of the news stations that Grandpa watched. The volume was all the way down, so Colt couldn't hear what the anchor was saying, but there was an image of Senator Bishop on the screen just over her shoulder.

"I didn't hear you come in," Grandpa said as he walked out of his office, startling Colt. His eyes were rimmed with red and his voice was heavy with emotion.

Looking at Grandpa was like looking at his own father. Sure, Grandpa was a few years older, but they had the same face, right down to the intense eyes. Both were tall and thin, but strong, with broad shoulders and ridiculously perfect posture, like they were always standing at attention. If Colt hadn't known better, he would have thought Dad was Grandpa's clone, not his son. It was eerie and comforting at the same time.

Grandpa walked over to the coffeepot and poured a fresh cup. He was a man of few words, and when he spoke it could be gruff. But Colt knew the real man—the man who had sat at his wife's bedside for months, reading Scripture or simply holding her hand as the cancer coursed through her body. He was a tireless advocate for military veterans, giving both his time and money. And he took Colt in when Colt felt like he had nowhere else to go. Sure, he could have stayed with one of his seven brothers, but they had lives of their own. They didn't need him underfoot, and since Grandpa was alone it seemed like a good enough fit.

"Are you okay?" Colt asked.

"You remember Senator Bishop?"

Colt nodded.

"He passed away tonight."

Colt frowned as he turned his attention to the television where they were showing footage of the senator and his wife at a political rally. Grandpa had been a friend of Senator Bishop's since they served together during the Korean War. The families remained close over the years, so Colt knew that news of the senator's death had to be hard on Grandpa.

"What happened?"

"According to the reports, he had a heart attack."

Something in his tone made Colt think that there was more to it. "You don't think it was an accident, do you?"

"I have my suspicions."

"But who . . . ?"

"That's the question now, isn't it?" He walked over to the living room and turned the volume up on the television just as the news shifted from Senator Bishop to the reactor leak in Iowa. Crews had been working around the clock to bring everything under control, but three of the contaminated workers had already passed away.

"Any more news about the virus?" Colt asked.

"Not much." Grandpa took a sip of his coffee. He had been one of the first recruits in the history of the CHAOS program, and even though he was retired, he still served as an advisor from time to time. That meant he had clearance to information that was off limits to most politicians and heads of state.

"I was thinking," Colt said. "What if it was Trident Biotech? I mean, they had the motive and the means to create something like that, right?"

"Possibly," Grandpa said. He sounded distracted. "I hate to do this—especially since you're leaving in a few days—but I need to go down to Tucson."

"Do you want me to go with you?"

Grandpa shook his head. "Not this time. I've arranged for you to stay over at the Romero house. You should be safe enough there until I get back. The way I hear it, they have a better security system than the White House."

After Grandpa left, Colt wandered back to his bedroom where weeks of dirty clothes covered every surface, hanging off the corner of the dresser, the doorknob, and the bed. He waded through the haphazard piles, trying to ignore the stench of mildew as he looked for something moderately clean to throw into his backpack so he had something for the morning. For the briefest moment he considered separating it into piles and throwing a load in the washing machine, but the thought didn't last.

As he packed, he grabbed his phone and a pair of earbuds before selecting a play list of country songs that reminded him of Lily Westcott. Colt had been smitten from the moment he saw her, though at first he tried to deny it. He didn't want to come across as shallow—after all, she was the consensus pick as the most beautiful girl at Chandler High School. She had blue eyes the color of cornflowers and blond hair that hung past the middle of her back. But it was her smile more than anything that had won Colt over.

The biggest hurdle to any kind of a relationship had been her boyfriend. Graham St. John was a walking cliché. He was tall and good looking, his parents had money, and he was an all-state quarterback who was heading to Boise State on a full-ride scholarship in the fall. He also cheated on her. But after she broke up with Graham, she and Colt never moved beyond friendship. Now that he was transferring to a military school in Virginia, they never would.

After a long search, Colt finally found some clothes that passed the sniff test. He wadded them up and stuffed them into his backpack, threw it over his shoulder, and was heading down the hallway toward the kitchen when something moved just outside the window. The hair on the back of his neck stood on end and his heart pounded, warning him that something was wrong. He forced his legs to cooperate, willing them to walk as he made his way to the bay window in the living room. A car door slammed, and before he could get a look at its driver, a black Mercedes CLS550 Coupe disappeared down the street and around the corner.

Colt opened the window, and there in the flowerbed were two footprints.

:: CHAPTER 9 ::

Oz lived with his parents in a sprawling house that looked more like a resort than a residential property. Surrounded by an iron gate with its own guardhouse, it had every amenity a person could desire, including an indoor basketball court, a movie theatre, a pool with a waterfall, and a gym that would rival any fitness club.

Colt stayed in the casita out back next to the pool, which was almost as big as Grandpa's house. It had a kitchen stocked with food, a dinette, two bedrooms, and an enormous living room with a projection television hooked up to just about every gaming system imaginable.

Oz ordered thin crust sausage and mushroom pizza from Papa John's, and the boys stayed up half the night playing Zombie Extermination Squad online with Danielle, who was back at her house lying on her bed with her dog, Wolfgang.

They decided to take a break around two in the morning. Oz flipped through the channels looking for something to watch, but by the time Colt got back from taking the empty pizza boxes to the trash bin, his host was snoring and cradling the remote like it was a security blanket.

Colt stumbled into the bedroom, plugged his phone in so it could charge for a few hours, washed his face, and fell into bed. The pillows were soft, like goose down, and he lay there staring at the ceiling.

He hated this time of the day more than any other. It was too quiet, the darkness too intimate. Daylight offered distractions like homework and chores, but at night he was stuck facing his thoughts.

Tomorrow would have been his parents' fortieth wedding anniversary, and the entire family had planned to celebrate together in Maui. Instead, Colt was packing up his life and transferring to a military academy on the other side of the country.

There were times it didn't seem real. Danielle said that was normal. The first stage of grief was supposed to be denial, but lately he had slid into the second stage. Anger.

At times he blamed God for everything that had happened, but maybe God didn't have anything to do with it. Maybe it was his mom's fault. After all, she didn't have to go public with her story. That's what a journalist did, of course, but was exposing Trident Biotech's secret mind-control program worth her life? Then there was Uriah Bloch, the guy who drove his truck into their car. There was also the doctor who implanted the chip into Bloch's head, not to mention Aldrich Koenig and about a dozen other people who played a part.

He thought about calling Lily, but it was too late. She had lost her parents before her second birthday and bounced around foster homes until the Westcott family adopted her. She was the only person he knew who truly understood everything he was going through. He was going to miss that when he moved to Virginia.

Colt's chest constricted with emotion, and he could feel the warm trail of a tear as it fell down his cheek. Angry. Sad. Frustrated, he whipped a pillow across the room. He wanted to scream or punch the wall or run and never look back. Instead he closed his eyes and fell into a fitful sleep, succumbing to his exhaustion.

⁙⁙⁙⁙⁙⁙⁙⁙⁙⁙⁙⁙⁙⁙⁙⁙⁙⁙⁙⁙⁙⁙⁙⁙⁙

The sun was already peeking through the slats in the blinds when Colt finally woke up. He groaned and turned over to find the alarm clock. It was almost ten, which meant that he'd missed his morning run with Oz. He lay there, finding the idea of sitting up almost more than he could bear. His mouth was stale, and it felt like someone was pounding at the back of his head with a rubber mallet.

"Are you up?" Oz called from the living room.

"No."

Before Colt could so much as blink, Oz was standing in the doorway wearing the same clothes he had fallen asleep in, as he shoveled spoonfuls of Fruity Pebbles into his mouth. "You want some breakfast?"

"Maybe later," Colt said, pulling the comforter over his head. Most people would have taken it as a sign to go away, but Oz either didn't get the hint or didn't care.

"Rise and shine," he said, sounding far too cheerful. Colt could hear him walking through the room, opening the blinds.

"I'll pay you a thousand dollars to go away."

"What are you talking about?" Oz asked as he sat down at the end of the bed. "I already let you sleep in. What do you say we head over to the shooting range, and if you ask real nice, I might let you shoot the 9mm Heckler or the MP5."

"You go," Colt said. "I'll meet you over there."

"Are you sick or something?" Oz asked as he pulled the comforter off the bed so Colt couldn't reach it. "How many people get a chance to shoot submachine guns? It's like we're living inside a video game."

"I guess."

"Are you going to tell me what's wrong or not? I mean, if you're hoping I can read your mind, I have news for you. I don't have telekinesis."

Colt yawned and rubbed his burning eyes. "Today is my parents' wedding anniversary."

"You should have said something."

"It's no big deal."

"You know, when Grandma Romero died, it was real hard on my dad," Oz said after sipping the milk from the bottom of his cereal bowl. "Don't get me wrong, I was sad and everything, but she had been battling cancer for as long as I can remember. In a way, we all had time to say good-bye. You didn't get that same chance with your folks." He paused. "I don't know what I would do if my parents were ripped out of my life like that."

Colt sat there, not knowing what to say. He was afraid that if he opened his mouth he'd start sobbing, and that was the last thing he wanted to do.

"I tell you what," Oz said as a smile crept across his lips. "I can't bring your parents back, but I may be able to do the next best thing."

:: CHAPTER 10 ::

Colt sat in what looked like a cross between a dental chair and a medieval torture device.

"You're sure those are necessary?" he asked, trying not to panic as the lab technician cinched a series of straps across his arms, legs, and chest.

"It's just a precaution." The technician was tall and thin, with skin the color of milk chocolate, a shaved head, and the kind of smile that could put people at ease. Unfortunately, it wasn't working with Colt.

As the technician checked the recording equipment, Colt wondered why he had let Oz talk him into this. CHAOS had patented an extraordinary technology that allowed them to extract human memories like a video recorder, complete with moving images and sound. Oz thought it would be a great way for Colt to capture important moments spent with his parents. That way he'd have access to them whenever he felt lonely.

It was a nice gesture, and Colt knew that Oz meant well, but he had been through this before. Thomas Richmond, a CHAOS agent, had visited Grandpa's house not long after Colt moved to

Arizona. He was hoping that some of Colt's memories would help identify the insider who had tipped off Colt's mom about Trident Biotech's mind-control program. When it was over, Colt had felt violated—like someone had recorded his innermost secrets. He wasn't sure he wanted to go through that again.

"I'm not trying to scare you or anything, but this is definitely going to hurt," the technician said as he fitted Colt with a series of sensors on his temples, forehead, and the back of his neck.

Colt closed his eyes and nodded, acknowledging that he had been fairly warned. "Do you have a name?"

"It's Tyreke," the technician said. "Tyreke Davis."

"I'm Colt."

"Yeah, Oz told me," he said, the smile never leaving his face. "So is it true? Is your granddad really the Phantom Flyer?"

"That's what people say."

"You know, I still have some of my comic books from when I was a kid."

"Get me out of here alive and I'll have my grandpa sign them for you."

"For real? My pops won't believe that when I tell him." Tyreke walked over to check the heart monitor, and then a machine with a series of dials and levers. "All right," he said. "This is your last chance to back out."

"I'm good," Colt said through gritted teeth, already anticipating the pain.

Tyreke flipped a series of switches, and the room filled with a loud buzzing sound. "Careful now. This is the worst part." He flipped another switch, and Colt felt a series of needles pierce his flesh under the sensors. His back arched as a wave of pain swept throughout his nervous system. Then his jaw clenched, and for a moment it felt like his body had gone into spasms.

Colt forced his eyes open to watch as a series of disjointed images flashed across a bank of monitors on the far wall. He could taste the saltiness of blood as he bit down on his tongue. Then the pain ended as quickly as it had begun, and he felt his body relax.

"You did great," Tyreke said as his fingers moved to unfasten the straps, but Colt noticed a shift in his mood. His smile was gone, and his eyes kept roving across the room like he was waiting for someone to jump out and grab them.

"How long did that take?"

"About five minutes, maybe less." Tyreke held what looked like an external hard drive. "I have special instructions to give you the master recording. You can watch it here or back at your place. Either way, it's yours to do with whatever you want."

"That thing has my actual memories?"

"Yeah, but you have to remember something. It doesn't mean any of it took place."

Colt frowned. "I don't get it."

"Your brain is filled with images that reflect reality the way you remember it. But let's say you witness an old lady getting mugged, and you fill out a police report. As far as you can remember, the guy who stole her purse was wearing a Yankees hat. But here's the thing—another witness swears it was a Red Sox hat. So who's right?"

"Couldn't you extract our memories and find out?"

"We could, but it wouldn't matter. Your version of the memory will trump facts every time."

Colt's eyes lit with understanding. "Meaning that no matter what, my recorded memory will still show the guy in a Yankees cap, even if the other witness was right."

"Exactly."

"Then how will I know what's real?"

"The parts that make you smile? Those are real. You can go ahead and delete the rest." Tyreke turned the hard drive over in his hands, and for a moment it looked like he was going to hand it to Colt. His smile disappeared, and he looked over his shoulder. "I only caught a glimpse of it, but one of your memories nearly sent you into cardiac arrest."

"You're serious?"

"How old are you, sixteen?"

Colt nodded.

"That shouldn't happen to someone your age, which means whatever it was, it was something crazy." He started to say something else, then stopped and slipped the hard drive into Colt's hand. "When something like that happens, we're supposed to log it and turn the recording over to the suits up top. But this meeting? It didn't happen. You catch me?"

"Not really."

"I did this as a favor because Oz is a cool cat—and it doesn't hurt that he's the director's son. He wanted me to take care of you, and I'm going to do that. But if this blows up in my face, I don't get fired—they send me to a labor camp in Siberia and then erase me from existence. My mom won't even remember that she had a son."

"So now what?" Colt had a sudden urge to be anywhere other than the lab.

Tyreke wrote something on a sheet of paper, folded it, and then handed it to Colt. "I know you came here hoping to capture a few memories of your folks, but you might want to start with this sequence first."

|||||||||||||||||||||||||||||||||||||||

Colt sat alone in the viewing room down the hall from the lab while Oz and Danielle waited in the reception area. He wasn't sure that he was ready for whatever Tyreke had captured with the memory recorder, but he knew that he had to watch. He unfolded the paper and found a series of numbers separated by colons, and he entered them into the playback system.

The screen flickered to life, showing Colt when he was six years old. He was sitting on an examining table in a small room with no windows. His parents were there, and so was Grandpa. It wasn't long before the door opened and a man wearing surgical scrubs with a CHAOS insignia over the chest walked in. He was short and a bit overweight, with thick arms covered in the same black hair that sprouted from his ears and the back of his collar.

"It's good to see you," he said, shaking Grandpa's hand. He did the same with Colt's dad, but his mom just nodded, her eyes focused on the floor instead of the doctor. The doctor smiled as he scruffed Colt's hair as though they had known each other for years. "So how have you been?"

"Okay, I guess," Colt said with a shrug.

"Do you know why you're here today?"

"Because you want to stick me with more needles?"

"Not this time," the doctor said with a broad grin. "I don't know how many people we've tested since this program began, but it's somewhere north of ten thousand. Each test has been negative, and to be honest, I didn't think that I'd see a match in my lifetime. In fact, I wasn't sure we'd ever get a match. Finding the right donor for a bone marrow transplant is hard enough, and that's between individuals who are the same species. Yet here we've been trying to find a human capable of hosting alien DNA. Do you know the odds for something like that to succeed? They're practically nonexistent."

"I think I'm going to be sick," Colt's mom said as his dad put his arm around her.

"Colonel," the doctor said, turning to Grandpa, "you helped start this journey almost sixty years ago, and I'm very proud to inform you that your grandson's DNA has successfully merged with a blood sample taken from one of the Thule. In fact, we've already received clearance to start the next stage of testing."

"He's my son, not some lab rat!" Colt's mom placed her hands protectively over his shoulders.

The doctor cleared his throat. "I understand that, ma'am," he said. "But your son? He's a miracle—an honest-to-goodness gift from above. And if everything progresses as we think it will, he could be the one to save the planet from those lizard men."

:: CHAPTER 11 ::

Colt was in a daze as he left the lab, unsure what to think. He knew that Oz and Danielle wanted to hear about the memories he recorded, but that was the last thing he wanted to talk about. He figured that they must have seen how upset he was, or maybe they didn't. Either way, he was thankful that they left him alone.

He sat in the backseat of the Jeep, looking at his hands as though they belonged to someone else. Was alien blood actually coursing through his body, or had the memories he watched been altered? Maybe, Colt thought, he had read about someone getting injected with alien DNA in a comic book or seen it in a movie. There had to be a logical explanation, because there was no way that the government was experimenting on kids.

He had Oz drop him off at Grandpa's house, where he ended up in front of the mirror, pulling at the skin on his face. As he checked his teeth and his ears, he wondered if it was some kind of mask hiding his true form underneath, but he didn't find anything out of the ordinary.

While he was in the bathroom, he heard the back door open

up as Grandpa walked in and plopped a bag of groceries on the countertop. Colt felt an anger rise inside of him. If those memories were real, it meant that Grandpa knew all along—and that he never said a word. How could he keep a secret like that? Colt wanted to shout, to punch something, but he settled for splashing cold water over his face.

"I thought you were going to lunch with your friends," Grandpa said as Colt walked into the kitchen. "Did they stand you up?"

"We need to talk."

Grandpa shut the refrigerator door and turned to look at Colt. "Okay," he finally said after an uncomfortable pause. "What seems to be the problem?"

Colt stood there as the emotion swelled. "I know."

"You're going to have to give me a bit more than that," Grandpa said as he took a stack of frozen chicken potpies out of a grocery bag.

"About the tests," Colt said. "The memories weren't false. I know what you guys did to me."

Grandpa placed the milk back into the bag. "Who told you?"

"It doesn't matter," Colt said. "Is it true? Did you let some guy shoot me up with alien blood?"

Grandpa reached for a handkerchief and blew his nose. "There's a bit more to the story, but I can't deny it," he said as he took a seat at the kitchen table. "You see, during the war the Nazis talked about an ancient Thule legend where the monsters believed their civilization was going to be destroyed by one of their own. I don't remember the exact word they used for it, but it translated to our language as the Betrayer."

"What does that have to do with me?"

"I'm getting to that part," Grandpa said, waving him off. "There was a guy in our platoon by the name of George Norman. Now, you had to know George, but one night he had too much to drink, and he came up with the crazy notion of injecting himself with some alien blood that he took from a cadaver. He figured that might make him one of them, and if that happened then he would become the Betrayer."

"That's ridiculous."

Grandpa shrugged. "He raided a medical supply tent, and before we knew it, a dozen of us were rolling up our sleeves to inject ourselves with the blood."

"You did it too?"

"We were desperate," Grandpa said. "But it didn't work. In fact, a couple of the men died, and the rest of us ended up in bed for a month. It wasn't too long before the U.S. Army assigned some of their top scientists to what they called Project Armageddon, a top secret program where they injected a few thousand GIs with a kind of serum that had alien DNA."

"And when that didn't work, they started shooting up a bunch a kids? How many died thanks to your little stunt?"

"More than I care to admit." Grandpa looked up at Colt, his lip quivering. "You don't know how much it hurt your folks to put you through those tests."

"It didn't bother them enough to stop it from happening," Colt said. "Why didn't you tell me? I mean, how could you keep a secret like that for all these years? Don't you think I had the right to know?"

"It wasn't my place. Your mom didn't want us to mention it until there was no longer a choice." Grandpa sighed. "Look, Colt, you may not want to hear this, but a lot of people are placing their hope in you."

"Why? Because they think I'm the one in the prophecy? Are you kidding me?"

"They've tested thousands of people over the years, and you're the only one who didn't reject the serum," Grandpa said, his voice heavy with emotion. "Like it or not, you're the one . . . the Betrayer."

"Yeah, right. That doesn't make me a hero, it makes me a freak!" He punched the refrigerator and stormed out the back door.

:: CHAPTER 12 ::

With nowhere to go, Colt ended up walking to Danielle's house. It was only a couple of blocks away, and her mother insisted on warming up a leftover chile relleno and some rice.

"Are you going to tell me what you saw in your memories today, or do I have to guess?" Danielle asked once they were alone in the backyard. "It must have been bad, because I've never seen you like this—not even after what happened with your parents. I seriously thought we were going to have to call a suicide prevention hotline."

"I'm going to ask you something, and I want you to be honest with me," Colt said.

"I'll try."

"I'm serious," Colt said. "You're the only person who tells me the truth anymore."

"What's going on?"

"Do you think I'm insane?"

Danielle started to laugh, but she stopped when she saw that he was serious. "You're not joking, are you?"

"You know something? I wouldn't be surprised if all of this came from my imagination—you know, what happened to my parents . . . the aliens . . . all of it. I could be lying in some mental ward in a medically induced coma right now while my subconscious makes everything up."

"Okay, now you really are scaring me."

Colt sat down on a patio chair near the pool and told her about the memories he had seen—how the government was running an experimental program on little kids, and how he was pretty sure some of them had died thanks to the injections.

"Do you want to know the crazy part?" he asked. "I'm the only one whose body didn't reject the serum. They think it means I'm some kind of chosen one. It just makes me a freak."

Danielle stood there staring at him.

"Say something already."

"Like what?"

"I don't know," he said, shaking his head. "Just tell me what you're thinking."

"The truth?"

"Yeah."

"The first thing I thought about was how hard it must have been on your mom. I mean, can you imagine what it would be like to watch your own child go through something like that?"

Colt couldn't believe what he was hearing. "She was there when it happened."

"Exactly," Danielle said. "I mean, fine. It's your life and you can be mad at her if you want, but what was she supposed to do? Hide you in a basket and send you down the river? Or maybe she could have sneaked you across the border and raised you in some remote South American jungle."

"I get the point."

"The second thing I thought about was how lucky you are."

"Are you serious?" he said. "For all I know, I'm going to sprout four more arms on my eighteenth birthday. I don't know about you, but that's not my definition of lucky."

"You're so busy feeling sorry for yourself that you're missing the point." Danielle crossed her arms. "When we were kids, I would get so excited when my parents told me that you were coming over. I'd pick a bouquet of flowers out of my mom's garden, and then I'd take all the chairs out of the dining room and line them up so we could play wedding."

"Is that why you always wore that white dress?"

"That only took you, what, ten years to figure out?" Danielle said. "You're a regular Sherlock Holmes."

"Look, I—"

"I'm not done," she said. "How many times did you walk down the aisle with me?"

Colt shrugged. "I don't remember."

"Well, I do," she said. "It was a grand total of zero, because all you wanted to do was play superheroes. You'd run around with a towel tied around your neck, pretending it was a cape. And if I didn't want to be your sidekick, I got stuck playing a super villain."

"How was I supposed to know? You never said anything."

"That's not the point," Danielle said. "You spent your entire childhood dreaming about saving the world from bad guys, and now that you have a chance to be a real hero, you want to pout and run away. I don't get it."

Colt was caught somewhere between disbelief and anger. "I don't want to run away, it's just that . . ."

"What?"

"I don't know," he said. "Maybe you're right."

"So what if you grow two more arms?" Danielle asked. "I mean, is that the worst thing that could happen? Besides, even if you do turn into one of the Thule, you can shape-shift into anything you want."

The beginnings of a smile played on his lips. "I guess I didn't think about that."

"Obviously," Danielle said. "And by the way, I have a secret of my own." She handed him an invitation that was stuffed inside a cream-colored envelope with gold foil lining—the same invitation that he had received a few weeks back.

"Are you serious?"

"Yep. I've been invited to attend the CHAOS Military Academy." Danielle was smiling so hard it looked like her cheeks were going to crack. "I couldn't believe it either! I mean, I wanted to go with you guys, but it's not like you can fill out an application or anything."

"When did you find out?"

"This afternoon."

"And you don't think Oz is playing some kind of practical joke?"

"What, you don't think I can make it?"

"It's not that," he said, instantly regretting the comment. "Have you told him yet?"

"No. I wanted you to be the first to know."

"I'm really glad, Dani," he said. "To tell you the truth, I didn't know how I was going to make it through the academy without you."

:: CHAPTER 13 ::

Morning came too quickly. The alarm went off at a quarter to six, and Colt hit the snooze button twice before he tried to unravel from his sheets. It was still dark, and everything inside of him yearned for sleep, but he knew Danielle would be up and ready to go.

Eventually he found a crumpled tracksuit and his running shoes, though he had to settle for mismatched socks. He thought about a shower, but there wasn't enough time, so he grabbed a baseball cap, slapped on some deodorant, and peeked through the crack in his door. He didn't want to run into Grandpa, who was usually up by now, but the lights were off and the house was quiet, so he grabbed his keys and went out the back door.

By the time he pulled into the parking lot, at the park Oz and Danielle were stretching in a grassy area next to the pond. Colt turned the engine off. Morning breath caked his mouth, but there was nothing he could do about it now. He would have to stop at a convenience store and grab some gum after their run.

"Good morning," Danielle said as he stepped out of the truck. "Are you feeling any better?"

"Not really." He stretched before getting distracted by a pair of ducks looking for bread crumbs.

"Let's go," Oz said, much to Colt's relief.

They set off at a comfortable pace, leaving the ducks to bother an old man who was tying a hook to the line of his fishing pole. Steam rose from Colt's mouth as he exhaled, his feet pounding the asphalt path as they followed a winding trail around the pond. There were tall trees and rolling grass all around. It felt like a wilderness trail instead of a park in the middle of a major city.

Colt's eyes fell to the scar on the back of Danielle's neck. Two weeks ago she'd had a biochip removed from the base of her skull. Aldrich Koenig, the imprisoned president of Trident Biotech, had ordered one implanted into her cerebral cortex, effectively turning her into a puppet forced to do his bidding. Koenig had done it to get at Colt, and it almost worked.

He blamed himself for what had happened, and even though she had forgiven him, he was still overwhelmed by guilt. He wanted to apologize again, to tell her he was sorry for getting her involved, but she had made him promise he would never say it again.

Colt slowed to a walk, his fingers locked behind his head as he breathed in through his nose and out through his mouth. The other two had disappeared around the corner, leaving him alone with his exhaustion. He closed his eyes and threw his head back, wanting nothing more than to crawl back into bed.

Something heavy moved through the trees. Birds took to the air, and Colt spun, his eyes wide as hair stood on the back of his neck. "Who's there?"

No response.

Each breath he took was amplified by the quiet. Colt thought about calling out for help, but his jaw wouldn't move. He heard leaves rustle and branches snap, and for a moment he thought that he could see a pair of eyes. Or was it his imagination?

There was a scraping sound, and he turned just as a woman rounded the corner with a black Lab in tow. Her cheeks were flushed, but she managed to smile as the dog sniffed at the trees. It growled and pinned its ears. "Come on," the lady said as she jerked the leash. The dog resisted as it tried to draw nearer to the shadows, but then it whimpered and ran after her.

Colt took off at a dead run, adrenaline driving his legs as he scampered down the path. Oz and Danielle were sharing a sports drink when he reached the parking lot. They decided to head back to Oz's house and grab some breakfast.

"If you want to leave your truck here, we can pick it up later," Oz said.

"That's okay. I'll just meet you over there." Colt watched them pull out of the parking lot before he fished his keys out. He went to open the door, but then stopped. Someone was standing behind him in the rearview mirror. Whoever it was, his eyes had a faint glow.

Tendrils of panic shot up Colt's stomach, making it difficult to breathe. His first instinct was to run, but where would he go? Instead, he opened the door and pretended to drop his keys. They clanked as he reached under the seat for Grandpa's tire iron, but by the time he spun around the figure was gone.

:: CHAPTER 14 ::

After a pit stop in the kitchen where Oz made everyone egg white omelets with turkey bacon, mushrooms, tomatoes, and spinach, he led them to a room that he called the arena. It was long and narrow, and the floor was covered in what looked like a wrestling mat.

"Here's the thing," he said as he slipped out of his shoes. "When you get to the academy nobody is going to take it easy on you just because you're a girl."

"Wait a minute," Danielle said. "What's that supposed to mean?"

Oz raised his hands in surrender. "Nothing, it's just that—"

"I don't expect you or anyone else to take it easy on me." Her words were sharp, her voice intense. "And I don't want either one of you treating me like I'm some kind of damsel in distress. Not now, and not when we get to Virginia. I earned that invitation, and I plan on proving it."

"Don't look at me," Colt said.

She stood there, feet planted and fists clenched until her knuckles were white.

Oz crossed his arms. "So that's the way it's going to be?"

Danielle blew at a loose strand of hair.

"Then let's get started." He opened with a basic fighting stance, showing Danielle how to bend her knees, place her left foot forward, and pick up her back heel. "Now raise your hands, but keep your elbows tight." He swung at her face and then her ribs, stopping before he made contact. "See? That's how you protect yourself."

Her eyes were wide as she nodded.

"Now, if you want to hit me back, you need to make a fist and lead with your top two knuckles." He took her hand and formed it into a first. Then he moved her arm so she struck the air next to his chin. "Remember, keep those elbows tight and pointed toward the ground. Then drive with your hips. You got that?"

"I think so."

"Show me." Oz stepped back and raised his palms, waiting for her to strike.

"You want me to hit you?"

"As hard as you can."

Danielle punched Oz with her left hand, then her right.

"Again, only this time remember to keep your elbows in and use your hips. Drive all the way through. That's where you get your power." He forced her to repeat it time and again, and it was obvious that she was getting frustrated. Her face was flushed as she threw punch after punch, grunting each time she struck his hands, but Oz just stood there, pointing out her flaws.

"Not bad for a newbie," he finally said after she threw a textbook combination. "If you keep it up, CHAOS is going to pull you off the hacker team and put you on the front line with the rest of us grunts."

A smile curled at the edge of her lips, and Colt thought she actually blushed. "Yeah, right."

The door opened, and a man with terra cotta skin and thick black hair walked in. He was tall with broad shoulders that were slightly hunched, as though he was carrying a heavy burden. But it was his eyes that gave him away. As Lobo smiled, they burned with intensity. Over the past few weeks, he had spent most of his time at the CHAOS headquarters in Virginia, which meant that this was the first time Colt had met him in person.

Oz crossed the floor and embraced his father. "I thought you were in London this week. What happened?"

"It's a long story, and I'm too tired to explain." Lobo held Oz at arm's length, pride pouring out of him like a neon sign on the Vegas strip. "We'll have plenty of time to talk at dinner, so why don't you introduce me to your friends?"

"This is Danielle Salazar," Oz said. "You know, the hacker I was telling you about?"

"Ah, yes. I hear there isn't a machine on this planet or any other that you can't access," he said. "I'm glad that my computer requires a biometric scan, otherwise your presence would make me nervous."

"It wouldn't stop her," Oz said.

Danielle blushed as Lobo frowned. "You're telling me that we've spent a fortune on our security, and it wouldn't matter?" he asked. "How long would it take you to break in?"

She shrugged.

"Don't be modest. Please."

"It depends," she said. "If I could lift a clean fingerprint, it should only take a few minutes. If not? I don't know. But there's always a back door. You just have to look hard enough, and you'll find it."

Lobo shook his head and smiled, somehow expressing admiration and disappointment at the same time. Then he turned his attention to Colt. "And you must be Murdoch's grandson," he said. His thick brows were furrowed, and his words lacked warmth. He didn't smile or offer his hand. Lobo simply stood there regarding Colt as if he were reading his thoughts . . . accessing his secrets.

:: CHAPTER 15 ::

Colt felt his body relax once Lobo left the room. He knew, even from their brief encounter, that the man was dangerous. He could see it in his eyes and in the way he walked. Each stride was purposeful, each step calculated. The very idea that Colt could somehow replace him seemed absurd. Colt wasn't even sure that he should have been invited to attend the CHAOS Military Academy, much less step in as the director of the entire organization.

"Let's have some fun," Oz said as he placed his hand on a biometric scanner. Green circles lit around his fingers and thumb as a portion of the wall slid away to reveal a room no bigger than a coat closet. Inside, a mechanical man stood at attention. The sleek machine was eggshell white, with a tapered chest and narrow hip joints. Its arms were long, as were its legs, and each of its hands ended in three wide fingers.

"This is an M-RC 4 Military Robotic Combat unit," he said, slapping it on the chest. "It's programmed to mimic over a hundred and fifty different fighting techniques." He entered a code into a tablet computer and its eyes flared to life. Its movement was fluid as it walked to the center of the room and took a fighting position opposite Colt.

"Check this out," Oz said. There was a whirring sound as a second set of arms unfolded from its back like a pair of wings. A third set opened up from its rib cage.

Colt stepped back. "You're kidding, right? I mean, how am I supposed to fight that thing?"

"If I were you, I'd start by putting my hands up."

Before Colt could react, the M-RC 4 lunged and struck him in the face with a combination of punches. His head spun left and then right before it snapped back from a quick jab. The flurry was over as quickly as it started. Colt stumbled as the robot went back to its ready position. Like a boxer knocked out on his feet, Colt was woozy. His knees wobbled, and it felt like the ground was slipping out from under him. He had to steady himself against the wall with one hand, but as he leaned over to catch his breath, he saw drops of blood. He wiped his nose with the back of his sleeve, leaving a streak of crimson.

"What are you doing?" he asked, his face twisted with anger.

"Look, McAlister. There's no such thing as a fair fight. I mean, what's going to happen if a shapeshifter grabs you by the throat? Call a time-out?" He laughed. "Give me a break. You can't afford to let your guard down, because the second you do, you'll end up six feet under."

Colt's nose throbbed as blood fell like crimson raindrops. He pinched the bridge, trying to stop the flow. It was swollen, and tears from pain filled his eyes. He wanted to lash out at Oz, but he couldn't—not when Oz was right. The world had changed. It wasn't a safe place anymore, and maybe it never had been. Either way, there was no room for error. Next time he'd be ready.

He pushed off the wall and made his way back to the center of the room, concentrating on each step as though he were walking on a tightrope instead of on solid ground. When he saw the shadow of the robot he stopped and took a deep breath. His knees bent, his right foot slipped back, and his elbows were in so that his hands covered his face.

"You ready?" Oz asked.

Colt nodded and bit his lower lip until he could taste the iron tang of his own blood. His body was tense, like a spring wound too tight, and he balled his hands into fists. He knew the odds of beating a six-armed machine were slim, but he was determined to land one blow before he went down.

"Fight!"

Colt led with his left hand and followed with his right, but the robot batted both away. Its eyes flashed as it brought two fists down on Colt's head. He managed to catch them, but the machine lashed out with two more arms. Air exploded from Colt's lungs as it struck him in the chest. He fell back, his head bouncing off the mat. His lungs refused to work and his body screamed for oxygen. He felt like a fish flopping around on the bottom of a boat, and when he opened his eyes, he saw the machine's foot drilling down at his chest.

Somehow Colt managed to roll away, and the robot missed, leaving an impression of its foot in the mat. Whether by instinct or training, Colt swept at its ankle with his leg and connected. Pain exploded in his shin, but the blow knocked the robot off balance.

He risked a glance at Oz, but Oz was too busy punching a set of commands into the computer. Another foot came crashing down, this time at Colt's head. He didn't have time to move, but he caught it with his hands. Sweat beaded on his forehead and veins popped out of his neck, but the machine was too strong. Colt imagined his head cracking under the pressure like an eggshell as his brains oozed across the floor.

"Can't you turn it off?" Danielle asked, her voice frantic.

"I'm trying," Oz said.

"Try harder! It's killing him!"

Colt wrenched his head to the right and rolled away. His chest was heaving, his energy tapped. "Isn't there . . . some kind of . . . kill switch?" Blood poured from his nose as sweat dripped down his forehead.

"It's not working."

"Just do something!" Danielle shouted.

The machine went for Colt, but Oz drove his fists into its back. It fell, and its arms and legs sprawled out like a dead insect. But it wasn't dead. A mechanical hand shot out and grabbed Oz by the ankle, pulling him to the ground.

"Get help!" Colt said, but Danielle just stood there, immobilized. "Now!"

Her eyes fell on him like she had just woken up from a nightmare, but she sprang to the door and grabbed the handle with both hands. "It's locked!"

The M-RC 4 was standing again, its eyes blazing as if it were somehow enraged. Its head swiveled toward Danielle for the briefest moment, but it must not have considered her a threat, because it turned back to Colt.

"How are we supposed to take it out?" he asked, sidestepping as the robot lunged. "Does it have a battery pack or something?" The machine swung its arm and hit him in the chest. He crumpled, but it caught him by the throat and hefted him against the wall. Its hand squeezed, and Colt's face turned red as fingers tried to pry the robot away.

Oz wrapped his arms around its neck, and it dropped Colt. The machine whirred until it took Oz by the shoulders and slammed him against the wall. Sheet rock crumbled, and he landed on his head with a thud.

With arms stretched wide, the robot turned on Colt and backed him into a corner.

"Dani, can you use that computer to hack into its operating system?" Oz asked.

"I . . . I don't know. Maybe."

Before she could move, the M-RC 4 dashed across the room, grabbed the computer, and snapped it in half. The monitor fizzled as pieces of plastic, glass, and wiring fell to the floor.

"Let's try Plan B." Oz managed to open a second closet where weapons hung neatly from hooks . . . rifles, submachine guns, and what looked like a pair of Tesla 6000 Electrostatic Repulsors. "Now would be a good time to duck." He grabbed one of the rifles and took aim. The air started to crackle, and Colt could feel his hair standing on end. He looked over and saw Danielle cowering against the door. Her lips were moving, but he couldn't hear what she was saying.

Oz squeezed the trigger, but the M-RC 4 fell backward. Its body bent at a ninety-degree angle as though it were dancing the limbo. Energy leapt from the barrel of the gun, but without a target it slammed into the wall as chunks of plaster exploded in a haze of white.

The machine leapt to the ceiling, hands and feet digging into the dry wall as it skittered across the surface like a spider. Oz fired again, and the blast ripped through one of its shoulder joints. A metal arm fell, but the ceiling caught on fire, triggering the sprinklers. Water fell and smoke plumed as the M-RC 4 hung upside down, its toes set deep into the ceiling. In one swift motion it ripped the rifle out of Oz's hands and tossed it across the room.

The weapon landed near Colt, and he didn't hesitate.

"Wait . . . what are you doing?" Oz asked. He fell to the floor, his hands covering the back of his head. Colt lifted the rifle, took a breath, and pulled the trigger. Sparks erupted as the robot's head flew from its shoulders. It bounced until it hit the floorboards, while the rest of its body fell on top of Oz.

Colt stood there with the barrel pointed at the lifeless machine as water dripped from his hair. "Can somebody tell me what just happened?"

⁙⁙⁙⁙⁙⁙⁙⁙⁙⁙⁙⁙⁙⁙⁙⁙

It had been nearly two days since someone hacked through the firewall and attached a computer virus to the M-RC 4's operating system. CHAOS investigators still hadn't been able to track down the hacker. The virus was elegant, subtle, virtually undetectable . . . and almost deadly.

At one point Danielle thought she had it contained, but when she ran a diagnostic of the entire network, it showed up everywhere. The virus had replicated and attached itself to executable files on dozens of programs, operating system files, and documents. Each was encrypted with a different key. By the time she deleted one, ten more would show up somewhere else.

Lobo was irate. CHAOS employed some of the most talented cyber experts in the world—former members of the FBI, CIA, and all branches of the military. Their lead architect set up the information security defense system for the Pentagon, yet despite their massive salaries and years of experience, none of them could answer how the hacker broke through.

"It was probably some punk at MIT trying to prove that he's smarter than our team," Oz said. "Stuff like that happens all the time."

"Maybe, but I realized something," Danielle said. "That thing was focused on Colt. I mean, when Oz tried to get in its way, it knocked him away and went back after Colt."

"Thanks for pointing that out," Oz said.

"Wait," Colt said. "You think that thing was trying to kill me on purpose."

"It's just a theory," she said.

"Dani might be on to something," Oz said. "I mean, you're the reason Aldrich Koenig is in prison right now. Maybe someone from Trident Biotech is after you."

:: CHAPTER 16 ::

Colt lay in his bed staring at the ceiling, earbuds pounding as he listened to a play list that was dominated by his dad's favorite singer, Johnny Cash. He had spent the better part of five days trying to figure out if someone was following him, and if they had anything to do with the attack at Oz's house.

He heard something outside his window, but when he looked, it was just the neighbor's dog barking at birds again. He fell back in bed and shut his eyes, unable to shake the feeling that someone was lurking just outside his periphery, watching . . . waiting. He wondered if the paranoia was a warning or if he was going crazy. Maybe it didn't matter. In less than twenty-four hours, he would be on an airplane headed to Virginia to start his new life. Again.

Cardboard boxes were piled high, some stuffed and sealed with packaging tape while others sat empty. Grandpa told him that he didn't have to pack up all his things, but Colt didn't see much point in leaving a mess. He was going to be gone for at least eighteen months, and after that—if he survived—he would likely end up at the Naval Academy in Annapolis or maybe at West Point.

Colt felt pangs of hunger in his stomach as he listened to Grandpa shuffling around the kitchen. According to the alarm clock, it was almost five. He was supposed to pick Lily up in about an hour, but he still hadn't taken a shower or even brushed his teeth. He was dragging his feet because he didn't want to let her go, and he knew that tonight was good-bye.

IIIIIIIIIIIIIIIIIIIIIIIIIIIIII

This year's rodeo felt more like a state fair. Beyond the bull riders and barrel races, there were carnival attractions, concerts, games, and dozens of vendors selling everything from glow sticks and belt buckles to deep-fried Twinkies and barbecue ribs. But that's not what drew the crowds, much less the reporters from around the globe.

In a joint effort with the newly formed Department of Alien Affairs, rodeo organizers had brought in several animal species from other planets. The DAA wanted to prove that the country didn't have to fear the unknown, so they created a program that would allow average citizens to interact with the strange creatures in a controlled environment. If everything worked out, there were plans for permanent exhibits at Sea World in San Diego, several of the Disney properties, and at least a dozen zoos and aquariums across the country.

There was even talk of creating an island resort where people could see the aliens in close approximations of their natural habitats, kind of like the Jurassic Park movies. Colt wondered if they were setting themselves up for the same kind of ending.

If the size of the crowd was any indication, the program was going to be a wild success. Colt had already seen a dozen people wearing T-shirts with little alien creatures on the front and a slew of kids carrying stuffed animals and action figures that weren't in any toy stores yet. Some had four arms, and others had nothing but wings where the arms should have been. There were cute creatures and gruesome monsters, colorful and drab, plump and stretched. But one thing was clear—they were all selling out.

"Look at that one." Lily smiled as a little girl squeezed some kind of teddy bear. It was round and covered in fur, but it had huge batlike ears, enormous eyes, and a button nose. "I wonder if it would make a good pet. You know, when they start to sell the real ones."

"It might look cute, but I bet that thing smells like an outhouse," Colt said.

The little girl, who wasn't more than five or six years old, stopped and stuck out her tongue. "I think *you* smell like an outhouse!" She ran after her mother, who was struggling to push a stroller through the mass of people.

Colt blushed, and Lily tried to hide her laughter. "I'm sorry," she said. "But you have to admit that wasn't very nice."

"It was just a joke."

"I can tell you never had sisters." She took him by the arm and led him into the crowd. "Come on, I want to see the exhibit, and I heard the lines are going to be crazy."

Bodies were pressed together as everyone tried to navigate beneath a forest of portable lights. They passed by a Ferris wheel and a stand selling kettle corn while the crowd roared in the grandstand behind them. Colt was sidestepping a clown who was twisting balloons into dogs and pirate hats when a man in overalls and a trucker cap barreled into him, spilling half of a frothing drink down the front of Colt's shirt.

"That was rude," Lily said.

"Excuse me?" The guy stopped. His brows creased over glassy eyes, and his nostrils flared. He was tall and broad, with rosy cheeks that looked more like jowls, and it looked like he was having a difficult time standing.

"It's okay," Colt said as the guy took an uneasy step toward him, his fists clenched. Colt tensed and raised his hands, palms forward, to show that he wasn't a threat. "Seriously, it's no big deal."

The drunken oaf sniffed, wiped his nose with his sleeve, and laughed. "That's what I thought," he said as he stumbled toward the grandstand.

"What a jerk." Lily rummaged through her purse, looking for a tissue to help wipe up the mess.

Colt shrugged. "Maybe, but look at this place. People are actually laughing and having a great time. Nobody's talking about the invasion or shouting that the end is near. If we have to put up with one drunk, then it's not so bad." He smiled and touched her arm. "Besides, I'm with you. And right now that's all that matters."

For a moment Colt thought that she was blushing. "We need to find you a new shirt," she said, and she headed to a tent where a vendor sold Western wear.

Colt walked alongside her, trying to memorize everything about her—the arch of her brow, the shape of her lips, the way her nose crinkled when she laughed. A picture wasn't good enough. Neither was a video. They were just reflections that captured a single moment in time. He wanted more than that . . . he wanted Lily.

She made her way through the booth, holding up a variety of shirts to see which she liked best. In the end, she picked out a black cowboy shirt with embroidered roses on the front and a skull on the back. She said it made him look like a rockabilly musician, and then she charged it to her dad's credit card. "I can use it for emergencies," she said after Colt protested. "And in my opinion, this qualifies. Besides, I didn't get you a going-away present."

"Thanks." Colt resisted the urge to brush a strand of hair from her eyes. He imagined the palm of his hand lingering on her cheek and then sliding down her neck, pulling her close to kiss her. Would she resist?

"What?" she asked, tilting her head.

If he was going to tell her how he felt, this was the time, but his chest clenched as the fear of rejection tore through him. "Nothing," he said, and then he went behind the tent to change.

By the time they reached the line for the exhibit, it was wrapped around an enormous building that looked like a cross between a tin shed and a barn. Intimidating men in dark suits stood at every door, while bizarre music echoed through a cluster of speakers that hung over the main entrance.

The air was heavy with the smell of fried bread and powdered sugar, and Colt's mouth started to water. He hadn't eaten since breakfast, which had consisted of only a granola bar and a glass of orange juice. He remembered seeing a booth where a man with a scraggly beard was selling corn dogs and funnel cakes, and he didn't think it was too far away.

"Are you hungry?"

"Starving."

Colt found the booth. While he waited for his turn to order, he looked up to the sky. The expanse of stars overhead reminded him of a fishing trip when his family stayed in a rustic cabin in northern Minnesota. He was young, maybe seven, and at night he'd lie in a hammock next to his mom. They'd look for constellations, and she would stroke his hair and sing to him. Eventually he would fall asleep, safe in her arms.

A news helicopter passed overhead, the rotors loud enough to pull Colt from his daydream. He closed his eyes, trying to grasp the image of his mom, but it slipped away. For a moment he forgot what she looked liked, and he started to panic.

"I think it's your turn," an elderly man said behind him.

"Sorry." Colt stepped forward, disoriented.

"How can I help you, son?" The man behind the booth was missing teeth, and the tattoos that covered his old arms looked self-inflicted.

Colt could hear the grease bubbling in the fryers as corn dogs and funnel cakes turned golden brown. He was about to place his order when the hairs on the back of his neck started to rise.

CHAPTER 17

Colt tried to appear inconspicuous as he looked over his shoulder, his eyes roving the crowd as he waited for the food. The line behind him had grown, but nobody stood out as a potential threat. There were no menacing glares, eye patches, or people with skull tattoos. Still, he couldn't shake the feeling that he was being watched.

The man behind the counter pulled a funnel cake out of the fryer and shook off the excess grease before he dumped it onto a paper plate and sprinkled it with powdered sugar. Colt thanked him and paid, dropping the change into a tip jar that smelled like pickles.

Between the corn dogs, lemonade, and the funnel cake, his tray was almost too full. Slowly, carefully, he made his way toward the condiment station to grab some napkins and a few packets of mustard. Then he stopped short. A man was standing in the shadows up ahead, hidden between two trailers. His eyes glowed dim against the darkness, just as they had the other morning at the park.

Colt felt paralyzed. The thrum of his heart pounded, and

in that moment he knew what it felt like to be hunted. His skin itched, his mouth went dry, and his eyes flitted as he looked for an escape route, but there was nowhere to run, no place to hide.

"Colt McAlister? Is that you?"

Startled, he turned to see a plump woman with a mess of blond hair that was twisted into a bun and held together by what looked like chopsticks. Her bangs were cropped short and streaked with pink, and her stylish glasses were perched on the end of her nose.

"Ms. Skoglund? What are you doing here?"

"I was about to ask you the same thing. I didn't know you were a rodeo fan." The school secretary, who also happened to be an undercover CHAOS agent, stood in the midst of the throng holding a cloud of pink cotton candy. She tore off a piece, popped it into her mouth, and licked the sticky sweetness from her fingers.

Colt glanced back to the shadows, but whoever had been standing there was gone.

"Is everything okay?"

"Oh, sorry." He forced a smile. "I thought I saw someone, that's all."

It was clear from the look on her face that Ms. Skoglund didn't believe him, but he didn't know what else to say.

"Look, I'm probably the last person on your mind right now, but there's something important I need to tell you, and I'm afraid it can't wait." She looked over her shoulder. "It won't take long, I promise. In fact, we can walk and talk if you'd like. That way your food won't get cold."

"Yeah, sure," he said, confused but intrigued. Had she come here looking for him?

"Just a minute." With a flick of her wrist, she tossed her cotton candy into a trash bin and reached into her purse for what looked like a ballpoint pen. She twisted it once and pressed down so it clicked. "That's better," she said as a small green light started to flash.

"What is it?"

"A little invention of mine." She smiled like a proud parent. "It's a kind of scrambler. You know, like a radar jamming device. If someone tries to record our conversation, all they'll end up with is static. That way we can keep things between us."

"Oh," he said, wondering why someone would care about their conversation enough to record it.

"What I'm about to tell you is probably . . . well, no, it's *definitely* going to sound insane, but if it wasn't true I'd be at home reading about hunky vampires instead of standing here at a rodeo." She paused, waiting for Colt to say something, but he didn't. "Okay . . . here it goes." She took a deep breath and exhaled slowly. "Someone inside CHAOS wants you dead."

Colt stopped, his face wrinkled in confusion as he tried to digest the words, but they didn't make any sense. She nudged him out of the way before a man pulling a wagon with three screaming children could run him over.

"Up until yesterday, I was the lead investigator on the security breach at the Romero house," she said. Her voice was low, and her eyes kept darting through the crowd. "Then I got . . . well, I suppose you would call it 'reassigned.' Apparently I started asking too many questions, but I'd already found this on Lobo's personal computer." She slipped a USB drive into Colt's hand. "There's a file called Operation Nemesis—as in the Greek goddess of revenge."

"Okay," Colt said, confused.

"One of the documents is a list of people who have been targeted for termination," she said. "Senator Bishop's name is on there . . . and so is yours."

Colt thought back to the day he came home to find Senator Bishop and Major General Robert T. Walker of the United States Army sitting at the kitchen table with Grandpa. He hadn't heard the entire conversation, but he got the gist. Washington wasn't happy with the direction that CHAOS was heading, and they were ready to make a change at the top. They wanted to replace Lobo with Colt . . . but was that reason enough for Colt to end up on some kind of hit list?

"So now what?" he asked. "I mean, it's not like I can call the police or anything. Are they even allowed to arrest people who work for CHAOS?"

"You have friends who will be looking out for you," Ms. Skoglund said. There was a loud buzzing sound coming from her purse, and she checked the display on her phone. Color drained from her face as she read the text message. "I'm sorry, but I really have to go," she said. "If everything works out the way I hope it will, then I'll see you soon."

"Wait . . . I'm leaving for Virginia tomorrow."

She winked. "I know."

Before he could ask what that meant, she slipped into the crowd and disappeared. He stood there trying to understand what had just happened. Then it hit him. If what she said was true, she had just risked her life to deliver that message.

:: CHAPTER 18 ::

Colt felt like a lamb in a den of wolves as he made his way back to Lily. Suddenly every face in the crowd was menacing, and everyone he walked past was a potential assassin.

By the time he reached Lily, she was huddled under a space heater at the front of the line. People grumbled as he slipped passed them with his tray in hand. He squirmed through the tight spaces and offered one apology after another, but it didn't help. The line was moving at a crawl, and everyone was anxious to get inside.

"I was beginning to think you'd left," Lily said.

"Sorry." He handed her warm lemonade and a cold corn dog as he explained how he had run into Ms. Skoglund, though he left out the part about Operation Nemesis. After a while the line started to move, and Colt tossed the soggy remains of the funnel cake into the trash.

"Come along then," said a woman wearing a jacket with a Department of Alien Affairs patch. She proceeded to go over the rules, which included no touching or feeding the animals. They weren't allowed to take any flash photography or stray from the path. Violators would not only be escorted outside the building, they would also face prosecution and likely incarceration.

"I wonder what would happen if we sneezed," Colt said.

"Stop it," Lily said, though she was smiling. "You're going to get us kicked out before we have a chance to see anything."

A set of double doors slid open, releasing a thick rush of wind that felt like summer in New Orleans. "This is incredible," she said, slipping out of her jacket as they entered a forest of exotic trees that rose to the vaulted ceiling high above.

They walked together down winding paths lined with flowers where the blooms were as large as heads of lettuce. Colorful birds flew among the branches, serenading everyone who walked below. There were spotted frogs with wings like dragonflies, red monkeys with four arms, and creatures that looked something like otters, though their bodies were covered in scales instead of fur.

Some of the handlers were actually aliens as well, and they drew as much attention as the animals. One had smooth gray skin and a long neck like a giraffe's, with an oval head and a cluster of four eyes that sat over its narrow mouth. He was a Fimorian, an elegant race of philosophers and artists, and he smiled politely as guests posed for pictures beside him. One little boy even asked for his autograph, and he was pleased to oblige.

"Will you take my picture with him?" Lily handed Colt her phone and ran over to stand next to the alien. Her head barely reached his shoulders, and Colt had to tilt the phone so the lens was vertical.

He was about to take the shot when the hairs on the back of his neck rose. His eyes roamed the floor as he looked for anything unusual, and then he saw it—a blur of motion. Someone in a suit and trench coat ducked through the service door.

Colt rushed over to check the lock and found the door open. "I'll be right back."

"Where are you going?" Lily's voice was a tense whisper. "It says employees only."

Colt slipped inside. An explanation was either going to scare her or make her think that he was crazy, so he decided it was best to say nothing at all. He just hoped that Lily was the only person who had seen him. The corridor was dark and cold and smelled like a dog kennel that hadn't been cleaned in a month. There was a cement block wall on his left, but on the right there was a series of windows that overlooked some kind of artificial ice cave where a creature that looked like a cross between a bear and a sloth paced back and forth.

Colt walked down the narrow corridor, hoping it didn't lead into the pen of some monster that liked the taste of human flesh. He knew he shouldn't be alone—that an assassin would want to separate him from a crowd so there were no witnesses. But it was too late to turn back now.

He looked over his shoulder to see the red glow of an exit sign above the door. Pipes groaned like the bowels of a ship, and something scampered across the floor. He heard a clattering sound, like a trash can being tipped over. Something brushed his shirt, and as he turned, someone grabbed him and threw him against the wall.

There was a loud crack as his head hit the cinder block, and for a moment he didn't know where he was. Someone hit him in the stomach. He fell forward and fists pounded his back, sending him to the ground. It was filthy, and he could taste the tang of slime on his lips.

Colt lay writhing, his entire body in pain as strong hands

grabbed him by his hair and pulled him to his feet. It was his only chance. He drove his shoulder into his attacker's stomach, picked him up, and slammed him to the ground. Quick as he could, he slid his right knee under the guy's left shoulder and his left leg under his neck, just as Oz had taught him. The attacker tried to push against Colt's chest, but Colt grabbed his arm and slid his right leg up over the man's head. He wrenched, completing the arm bar, and the man screamed in pain as his elbow joint threatened to pop.

"Who are you?" Colt asked, grimacing as he applied more pressure. He looked down to see eyes that glowed in the half light of the corridor. They belonged to a handsome man wearing a tailored suit.

"I'm your worst nightmare come true."

Colt frowned as the man's face morphed. Skin and bone stretched to form a long snout, shifting from soft pink to a rough green. The fabric of his jacket ripped away as two extra sets of arms grew out from its back and a tail slapped against the cement floor like a hammer. It was one of the Thule.

The door at the end of the corridor opened and light flooded the darkness. Colt turned to see Lily. Her arms were wrapped around her shoulders and she looked frightened, but someone pushed past her and she was gone. A man in a dark suit and fedora, his strides long as raced toward Colt and the monster, shouted, "Don't move!" and raised a Glock 22 with a light mounted under the barrel.

More agents burst through the door as the Thule wrapped a massive hand around Colt's face and threw him against the wall. There was a cracking sound as the back of his head smashed against brick. Colt fell, dazed, as the agents drew near. He opened his eyes long enough to see the DAA badge hanging from the belt of the first man.

"Put your hands in the air, now!" the agent said.

The Thule hissed before it turned to run. The agent fired, and light flashed as an explosion echoed against the walls. Frightened animals howled, but Colt couldn't hear anything except a high-pitched whine, like the feedback when a microphone gets too close to a speaker. Two more shots rang out, and though he was disoriented, Colt watched the monster slip out the back door and into the night.

:: CHAPTER 19 ::

Colt had wanted the night to be memorable, but it looked like it was going to be memorable for all the wrong reasons. He stood handcuffed in the shadows of the doorway, his head swimming. The animals inside their cages filled the air with their discordant cries, like a symphony orchestra warming up before a performance.

Agents from the DAA were in the process of clearing the exhibit floor, but it wasn't an easy task. Frustrated patrons had waited in line too long to be swept away without explanation. A heavy man wearing a crooked toupee demanded the badge number of another agent. "You'll hear from my lawyer," he said, his face red and his forehead beaded with sweat. "I have rights, you know."

The agent standing next to Colt had a pointed nose and a strong jaw that was shaved as clean as his scalp. His eyes were intense and his brow furrowed as he watched the commotion from beneath the brim of his fedora. He wasn't holding his gun any longer, but Colt could see the bulge under his suit coat.

"Look, I know I shouldn't have been back there, but if you

would just let me explain," Colt said, but it was a waste of time. The agent refused to acknowledge him, much less look at him. Colt looked around for Lily.

"All right, let's go." The agent grabbed Colt's arm and led him across the exhibit floor. Most everyone had been evacuated, but lights flashed as someone wearing a press credential took several pictures of Colt before another agent stepped between them. Colt had a feeling he was going to end up on the front page of the morning paper, or worse—all over the Internet on news sites and blogs.

"Will you at least tell me what I'm being charged with?"

"For starters? Trespassing, which is more than enough to hold you for as long as it takes."

"What about my friend?"

The agent smiled, his first sign of emotion. "She's been detained for questioning."

"But she didn't do anything."

"Then she won't have anything to worry about." The agent pulled Colt down a hallway, through a door, and into a cramped room that looked like some kind of temporary office space. The walls were bare, with the exception of a calendar that hung above an empty desk. There were three chairs and a filing cabinet, and that was it.

"Take a seat," the agent said, pushing Colt into the nearest chair.

He stumbled, wrenching his bruised shoulder as he fell back. His vision was still a bit blurred and his head pounded from the creature's slamming him against the cinder block wall.

"Do you have any aspirin?" Colt asked, but the door opened before the agent could answer.

A thick man who was unexpectedly short walked into the room carrying a briefcase and looking harried.

"Sorry to keep you waiting," he said as he set his briefcase on the desk. "I trust you've been introduced to Agent Parks." He nodded at the agent, who was now standing in the far corner.

The man removed his fedora, smoothing out hair that was wringed with sweat. "My name is Agent Hester, and I'm with—"

"The Department of Alien Affairs," Colt said. "Yeah, I saw the badge."

"Very good," Agent Hester said as he flipped the briefcase open. "Can I get you anything? Water? Coffee?"

"I was just asking Agent Parks for an aspirin," Colt said.

"Well, that shouldn't be a problem." He turned around to face Agent Parks. "You wouldn't mind, would you? Oh, and on your way out, could you remove the handcuffs? I don't think we'll be needing those any longer."

Agent Parks hesitated, though only for a moment. Colt thought that he saw a sneer cross the man's lips. He had a feeling that Agent Parks minded very much, but he did as he was asked and removed the cuffs before leaving the room in search of the aspirin.

"Better?" Agent Hester pulled back his jacket to adjust his waistband, and as he did, Colt saw the Glock 22 that hung from a holster on his hip.

"Yeah, thanks," Colt said, rubbing at his wrists. The two agents couldn't have been any more different, and it wasn't just their appearance. Agent Parks was intense, but Agent Hester was kind, almost gentle. It was the old good cop, bad cop routine that Colt had seen in dozens of movies, and he wasn't going to fall for it.

"I'll admit that when I got the call, I was surprised to hear who we had in custody," Agent Hester said as he opened a manila folder and leafed through the pages. "I mean, what with your saving the world from those nasty lizard men, I feel as though I should be offering my sincerest gratitude, but . . . well, here we are."

There was a long pause as he stopped at a sheet of paper, his pointer finger going over each line carefully as his eyes roved back and forth. "You realize, of course, that you have placed your position as a cadet at the CHAOS Academy in jeopardy." He flipped the folder shut and tossed it into his briefcase. "They have strict rules when it comes to admittance, and I'm afraid a felony trespass won't do you any favors."

Colt fidgeted in his chair. This was ridiculous. All he did was sneak into the feeding area of some intergalactic zoo. How was that a felony?

"Of course if you cooperate with our investigation, I might be able to help . . . though I can't make any promises. You understand."

Not really, Colt thought. He didn't understand at all. "What investigation?"

Agent Hester pulled a metal disc from his briefcase and set it down on the desktop, just in front of where Colt was seated. "You wouldn't happen to know who this is, would you?" he asked. With the click of a button, a hologram flared to life. It was a perfect three-dimensional replica of the man Colt had chased into the corridor, though he was only about the height of a ruler, if that. He stared at it for a moment, not sure what to say. For all he knew, Agent Hester was in on everything. His eyes went from the hologram to the gun and then back to the hologram. "It's the guy who was following us tonight," he finally said.

"Interesting." Agent Hester scratched his chin. "His name—at least so far as we know—is Heinrich Krone. He's a former member of Germany's federal intelligence service, who is currently working as an assassin for hire. And he's also one of the Thule, as you recently discovered. But I'm sure you knew all this already."

Colt frowned. "No, I didn't." He thought back to what Ms. Skoglund had told him. As much as he didn't want to believe that someone at CHAOS wanted him dead, things weren't looking good.

"I see." Agent Hester stared at Colt through his glasses as though he were a human polygraph machine. "Then you had no idea that he is one of the Thule, or that he had a known relationship with Aldrich Koenig, the former president of Trident Biotech? Or that he has received multiple payments from accounts associated with the Central Headquarters Against the Occult and Supernatural?"

"Look, all I know is that we came here to see the exhibit and some creep started following us," Colt said, sitting back in the chair. "I didn't know who he was, so when I saw him slip behind the door, I decided to get a closer look. The next thing I know, someone slams me up against the wall, and then one of your agents points a gun at my head. The guy who hit me gets away, and somehow I'm the one who ends up in handcuffs."

The door opened, and Agent Parks walked in carrying a small bottle of aspirin and a glass of water, which he handed to Colt. "We're going to have to let him go," he said as though the words were bile in his mouth.

Agent Hester looked confused. "Excuse me?"

"The bureau chief just got a call," Agent Parks said. "The kid has friends in high places."

"Apparently so." Agent Hester looked crestfallen.

"His grandfather is on his way to pick up him up, and from what I've been told, he ain't happy. You know who he is, right?"

Agent Hester nodded. "Yes, yes. The Phantom Flyer, America's one true superhero. I read the comics when I was a boy."

Colt felt the tension leave his body as Agent Hester paced with his fingers locked behind his back. His neck was a peculiar shade of red that crept up his cheeks and onto his forehead like the rising temperature on a thermometer. Colt couldn't tell if he was embarrassed or upset, though he had a feeling it was a bit of both.

"This certainly complicates things, doesn't it?"

"Does that mean I can go?" Colt asked as he stood up.

"Yes, I suppose it does," Agent Hester said. "But before I forget, we found this in the corridor." He pulled Ms. Skoglund's flash drive out of his breast pocket and handed it to Colt. "I don't suppose you'd like to make any comments about Operation Nemesis? Or why your name shows up on a list of people who are no longer alive?"

CHAPTER 20

By the time Colt was released, Lily was already gone. Her father had picked her up and taken her home before Colt had a chance to say good-bye, much less explain everything that had happened. Maybe that was a good thing, Colt thought. After all, he wasn't sure if he could explain it even if he had the chance.

Agent Hester led Colt out of the office and back to the exhibit area where Grandpa was talking to an older man. He was tall and slender, with perfect posture, and his sun-bronzed skin was a striking contrast to his impossibly white hair.

"I hate to interrupt, but . . ." Agent Hester let the words hang in the air as Grandpa and the other man turned to them.

"You must be Colt," the man said. "It's a pleasure." He offered his hand, which was soft and smooth, as though he frequently applied cream. Yet despite that and his manicured fingernails, his grip was strong.

"This is Agent Montgomery," Grandpa said by way of introduction. His tone was even, but his eyes were furious. "He's the local bureau chief for the DAA."

"Nice to meet you," Colt said.

"I wanted to personally apologize for our overzealous behavior tonight." Agent Montgomery applied a smile that looked like it was stolen from the face of a used car salesman. "As you can imagine, my agents have been through quite a lot these last few weeks. Still, it doesn't excuse the terrible mix-up. I hope you'll be able to forgive us."

"They were just doing their jobs." Colt looked over his shoulder at the exit sign. Agent Montgomery gave him the creeps. Besides, he wanted to at least text Lily to see if she was okay.

"Thank you," Agent Montgomery said. "You'll be happy to know that we confiscated the pictures that were taken earlier. You know, the ones that showed you in a bit of a compromised position?"

"I appreciate that," Colt said, almost dismissively. He didn't want the world to see him in handcuffs, but he had bigger issues at the moment. "Did you find the guy who attacked me?"

"The shapeshifter?" Agent Montgomery looked over to Agent Hester, who shook his head. "I'm afraid not, though we have some of our best agents tracking him right now. With any luck, he'll be apprehended within the hour and we'll be able to get to the bottom of this mess."

"Then we'll leave that in your capable hands," Grandpa said. He placed his hand on Colt's shoulder and steered him toward the exit sign.

"Oh, and, Murdoch," Agent Montgomery said, calling after Grandpa. "Please contact me if you see anything unusual. You have my direct line."

"I'll be sure to do that."

"Do you know that guy or something?" Colt asked as they got into Grandpa's 1946 Cadillac Coupe. The car looked like a hot rod, with a long front end, a chrome grill, and black paint that shone beneath the portable lights in the parking lot.

"Agent Montgomery?" he asked with a snort. "He used to work for CHAOS."

"What's his deal?"

"He's what you might call an opportunist." Gravel crunched under the tires as he pulled out of the parking spot, headlights cutting through the darkness. "In his world justice comes secondary to publicity and promotion. But I'm not worried about Montgomery right now. I want to know how long that thing has been after you."

His tone was harsh, and Colt shrank back into his seat like a puppy that had been scolded for chewing up a pair of slippers. "I don't know."

"Don't give me that," Grandpa said as he looked into the rearview mirror. "The Thule secrete a kind of fear toxin that paralyzes their victims. You start to panic, your skin gets covered in gooseflesh, and the hair on the back of your neck stands on end. Sound familiar?"

Colt shrugged. "Yeah, I guess," he said. "The first time I noticed anything was the other day when you went down to Tucson. I was in the hallway, and it felt like someone was watching me from the front window. Just like you said, the hair on the back of my neck stood up and I could hardly breathe." He went on to explain how he saw the glowing eyes in the rearview mirror at the park and how the robot flipped out at Oz's house and nearly killed him. Then he repeated everything that Ms. Skoglund had told him.

"That much I knew," Grandpa said, to Colt's surprise. "She stopped by the house after you left, and I told her where you were. If I had known you were going to go chasing after trouble, I would have had her bring you home."

"Trust me, that won't happen again."

"We'll see about that," Grandpa said. He turned the dial on the radio until it played big band music. "So, tell me, who else knows about this mess?"

Colt shrugged. "Nobody, really. I mean, I guess Ms. Skoglund does, but that's it."

"You haven't said anything to Danielle or Oz?"

"Not yet. I mean, what would I say? It's not like I had any proof." Colt tried to let it all sink in, relieved that he could finally talk to someone. "Do you really think someone from CHAOS is trying to kill me?" He paused. "You know, like Lobo?"

"Lobo came from a rough background. His father was shot when he was young, and his mother dealt and abused drugs, so she spent a good deal of time in and out of prison. Without good role models, he got involved with gangs. In fact, the only reason he joined the service was to avoid a prison sentence, but eventually he got his act together. The man worked harder than anyone I know, but he was overlooked for promotions because the top brass couldn't look past that rough exterior. Still, he never gave up. In fact, it only made him work harder. He fought for every scrap, and now that he's the director of CHAOS, he's not going to go down without a fight." Grandpa sighed. "I told them this would happen, but they insisted on privatizing the agency and putting him in charge." He shook his head. "Fools."

Colt watched as the desert landscape blurred outside his window. The hum of the tires rolled over the asphalt as he mulled his future. He was about to enter into a military training program where the director of the agency wanted him dead. It didn't seem like a terribly good idea on any level. "What's going to happen," he asked. "I mean, should I even go to Virginia?"

"Ultimately that's a decision only you can make," Grandpa said. "You were put on this earth for a purpose, and it's up to you with the good Lord's help to discover what that is. But you need to understand that there's nowhere you can hide that Lobo won't be able to find you."

There was a sound like an engine, and Colt looked in the rearview mirror to see a single headlight dart between an SUV and a semi-trailer truck. The rider on the back of the motorcycle revved the throttle, and the front tire pulled off the asphalt. He was going fast enough that if he hit a patch of gravel, he wasn't going to survive the crash—even with the helmet.

Colt watched as the motorcycle drew near. The front tire touched back down, bouncing twice. Colt frowned. The rider had six arms instead of the normal two, and he was holding four handguns with long, silver barrels—all of them leveled at the Cadillac. "Grandpa, look out!"

There was a series of flashes followed by explosions. The impact from the energy bolts shook the car, and the back end swerved out of control. There was a scorch mark like a starburst on the window, but it didn't shatter. In fact, there wasn't even a crack.

"I've added a few upgrades," Grandpa said. "The glass is bulletproof."

Grandpa fought to maintain control as the SUV behind them veered off the road and into the guardrail. Cables snapped and the front end crumpled as steam rose from what was left of the hood.

There was another series of shots. Three flew overhead, but one of them caught Grandpa's bumper. "Hang on!" He slammed his foot against the brake pedal, and the car lurched as they swerved and skidded across the freeway, leaving a slithering trail of rubber in their wake. The seat belt dug into Colt's skin, but without it he would have flown out the front window.

"Looks like your friend found us before Agent Montgomery and his crack staff were able to track him down," Grandpa said as the motorcycle flew past them in a blur of motion.

The rider, whom they assumed was Krone, applied the brake and turned back around just as Grandpa pressed the gas. The force from the acceleration slammed Colt's head against the seat.

"Sorry about that," Grandpa said as he reached for a hidden panel in the dashboard. It eased open to reveal a series of gauges, levers, and switches. "Do you see that white one next to the red button? Flip it on."

Colt did as he was told, and two wide panels opened on either side of the hood just above the front tires. "No way," Colt said as a pair of Gatling guns emerged. "When did you install those?"

"A week or two before you arrived," Grandpa said. "Let's just hope they work."

They raced toward the motorcycle in a deadly game of chicken. Grandpa pushed a white button and the guns blazed to life, smoke billowing from the barrels as bullets shredded the asphalt.

Cars and trucks pulled to the side of the road, their drivers stunned as they watched the quiet stretch of freeway turn into a war zone. Some remained in their vehicles, others got out to get a better look—and some of them had cameras.

Krone fired. Energy blasts bounced off the grill of the

Cadillac, but Grandpa kept driving, the Gatling guns blazing as bullets sprayed the motorcycle. Flames erupted near the gas tank, and the front tire started to wobble. There was an explosion, and Krone flew off the back, arms and legs flailing as the motorcycle skidded across the freeway in a shower of sparks and flame.

Grandpa took his foot off the gas and eased his way to where Krone should have landed. Sirens screamed in the distance.

Colt stepped out of the car, but he couldn't find the Thule assassin anywhere. "That's crazy," he said, standing in the head-light beams of the Cadillac. "He just disappeared."

:: CHAPTER 21 ::

It didn't make sense. Krone should have been lying on the asphalt in a tangled heap, either unconscious or worse. At that speed bones would break and organs would be lacerated, if not rearranged, but there was no sign of him anywhere. No skid marks, bloodstains, or even footprints leading off into the desert.

The only explanation Grandpa could come up with was a personal teleporting device. Such things were rare, and highly unstable, but they were supposed to open a gateway that could take someone from one point to another instantaneously. Travel distances were limited, typically to somewhere within a line of sight, but it would have been enough for the Thule assassin to escape.

A stream of patrol cars with flashing lights cut the search short. They got back into the car, but before they took off, Grandpa reached inside the glove box and pulled out a metal orb about the size of a baseball. "It's an EMP grenade." He spun a dial counter-clockwise until there was a click, then he pressed a button, and a blue light started to pulse. "It should scramble any recording device that managed to take our picture without hurting anybody in the process. That way we can stay anonymous."

"Anonymous?" Colt laughed. "How many people drive a '46 Cadillac Coupe? And then there are the retractable Gatling guns. It's not exactly a good car for sneaking around."

"Don't worry about that," Grandpa said as he dropped the grenade out the window. It landed with a *tink*, bouncing a few times before it came to rest. "We need to get out of the blast radius before it kills our battery." He threw the car into drive, and the tires spun before the vehicle shot forward to an off ramp that led back into a neighborhood.

Colt watched through the rearview mirror, waiting for the grenade to detonate. There was an explosion of crackling light as energy waves rippled across the freeway like water disturbed by a heavy stone. Headlights dimmed as the pulse fried streetlights, batteries, and anything else that used electrical components.

In the distance the first patrol car entered the electromagnetic field. Its lights flickered and siren sputtered before they went out, then the engine ground to a halt. The same happened to a second patrol car before a third driver slammed on his brakes and rear-ended the first. The first highway patrolman staggered out of his vehicle, his hand moving to the radio transmitter on his lapel.

Grandpa drove home using side streets. He wanted to avoid major intersections where cameras hung from traffic lights, feeding live footage to the watchful eyes of the police department. They were only a few miles from home, and it wasn't long before he pulled into the driveway and cut the lights, keeping the car in idle as Colt got out to open the garage door.

"I don't get it," he said. "You have an armored car that could take out a tank, but you won't buy a garage door opener?"

"It's good exercise," Grandpa said as the garage door slid open. He eased the car inside, and Colt shut the door before he flipped on the bank of fluorescent lights that hung from the exposed rafters.

Grandpa got out and inspected the car. Surprisingly, there weren't any dents, much less any dings or scratches. But there were some nasty-looking scorch marks left by the charges that Krone had hit them with. He walked over to an old cabinet and pulled out a rag and a spray bottle filled with some purple liquid, handing both to Colt.

"What's this for?"

"The evidence," Grandpa said. He hit a button on his wireless remote, and the license plate spun backward, replaced with a brand-new number.

"I didn't know you were this devious."

"Never mind," he said. "You have work to do."

Whatever it was, the compound in the spray bottle was powerful. In only a few minutes the scorch marks came right off without damaging the paint or the chrome on the grill.

"So do you have any more secret weapons stores that you want to tell me about?" Colt asked as he put the cleaning solution away. "Is there some kind of hidden lab under the house, or do you keep all that stuff in a storage facility somewhere?"

"Lock the door, will you?" Grandpa said as he walked back to the house. When he got inside, he hung his keys on the hook and opened the junk drawer, where he rifled through pens and pencils, mismatched batteries, expired coupons, and spools of thread. "Here it is," he said, pulling out something that looked like a remote control, only it was nearly the size of a paperback novel and had a stubby black antenna on the end. He twisted a dial and a meter sprang to life, bouncing back and forth across the display as the device made an annoying crackling sound.

Colt thought it looked like a handheld version of the metal detectors that old men use to comb beaches in search of spare change. "Are you going to tell me what you're doing, or is it top secret?"

"I'm looking for hidden wires," Grandpa said as he scanned the countertops, walls, and even the ceiling. "I need to make some calls, and I don't want anyone listening in."

"How old is that thing?"

"About as old as I am, but it works better than the cheap gadgets they build today." Grandpa's eyes were focused on the meter as the needle continued to bounce. When he was finished with the kitchen he went through the family room, then down the hall and into the bedrooms. He even checked the guest bathroom.

"Don't forget to look under the plunger," Colt said as he grabbed a bag of frozen peas from the freezer and walked over to the sofa. The peas were for his head, which was still pounding despite the aspirin Agent Parks had given him. He walked into the living room and picked up the remote control, flipping through the channels until he landed on a news station. The phrase *Late Breaking News* was splashed across the bottom of the screen as they showed live footage of a freeway that looked like it had been bombed. The asphalt was chewed up, and cars lined the road haphazardly while people milled about in confusion.

"Hey, Grandpa, you're going to want to see this," Colt called over his shoulder. "It looks like we made the news."

The door to the office clicked open and Grandpa walked out, his reading glasses perched on the end of his nose as he stood behind his favorite chair. Images continued to flash. They showed the patrol cars piled up, the smoking SUV crumpled against the railing, and a close-up of the motorcycle in the middle of the freeway.

"Despite the devastation, there were no serious injuries, though one driver was treated by emergency workers for minor lacerations," a reporter said. "Witnesses claim one of the suspects dropped a grenade, releasing a burst of electromagnetic radiation. It effectively destroyed any electrical equipment within the blast radius, which explains all the dead car batteries and streetlights."

The image on the screen changed to a helicopter with a floodlight that roved across the desert floor as K-9 units searched the area. "Two of the suspects fled in a black two-door sedan, while police continue to search the outlying area for the person who was riding the motorcycle," the reporter continued. "At this time it is not known if any of the suspects were extraterrestrials."

"Now what?" Colt said as he turned the volume down.

"I wouldn't worry too much about it," Grandpa said. "It'll be old news by morning." He went back to the office without another word, leaving Colt alone with his thoughts and the remote control.

Colt looked out the window, wondering if Krone was watching him from the shadows or if the hit man was hidden from sight trying to recover from his injuries. Even if he managed to teleport away before he hit the pavement, Colt doubted that would have slowed his momentum. He was flying off the back of the motorcycle, which meant when he came out the back end of the portal he probably landed on a cactus or a rock.

He started to close the blinds when a car pulled up to the curb across the street. The driver was human, or at least he looked human, but the thing in the passenger seat was definitely a machine. It was covered in metal plating, and it had a single eye that glowed faintly blue in the darkness.

:: CHAPTER 22 ::

Colt rolled his eyes. The driver was none other than Thomas E. Richmond, the same CHAOS agent who had extracted Colt's memories not long after he moved to Arizona. His partner was D3X, an advanced military robotic unit with hands that morphed into plasma cannons. Colt had seen it in action during the skirmish at Trident Industries, where D3X took out Thule warriors as if they were garden gnomes.

"Were you expecting visitors?" Colt asked the question loud enough that Grandpa could hear him through his office door.

"I asked Agent Richmond to keep an eye on the house until things settle down a bit. Why, is his car out front?"

"Unfortunately."

"Do me a favor and start a pot of coffee, will you?"

"Does that mean you trust him? Because—"

"Just make the coffee."

Before long, the distinct aroma of coffee grounds permeated the kitchen, and as the water percolated, Colt decided to lie down on the couch. The frozen peas stung his neck, but the cold brought some welcome relief to his pounding headache. He looked at his cell phone on the coffee table and wondered if he should call Lily. She was probably upset, and he was sure that her parents were furious. The problem—at least as far as Colt saw it—was that if he didn't call to check up on her, it was going to make him look like an even bigger jerk. Resigned to his fate, he reached for the phone, but before he could dial her number, the phone beeped twice. According to the display, it was a text message from Oz.

He was about to open it when a thought popped into his head. There was a good chance that Oz knew something about Operation Nemesis. After all, he was always accessing files that he wasn't supposed to see. So did that mean he knew that his dad had killed all those people? And that he was trying to kill Colt?

Colt tapped the video chat icon and selected Danielle's name. He needed to sort everything out, and it was looking like she was the only person he could trust. When she answered, a video showed up on Colt's display. She was sitting on her bed, and her eyes were red and puffy as her Pomeranian tried to lick her face.

"Are you okay?" he asked.

"I just got back from dinner with my parents, and I can't stop crying," she said, her voice shaky. "I don't know . . ." She paused to take a deep breath. "Maybe I shouldn't go with you guys tomorrow. I mean, what was I thinking? We're going to be gone for what? Eighteen months? That's an eternity. Besides, Oz probably had to beg his dad to let me in."

"Yeah, right," Colt said. "You have a gift . . . of course it's a gift for breaking into other people's computers and stealing their data, but it's still a gift."

"I guess," she said. "How did everything go with Lily? Are you guys . . . you know, official?"

"Because that makes a lot of sense. It's not like I'm moving away tomorrow or anything." He sighed. "Besides, after tonight I don't think she'll ever talk to me again."

"Yeah, right. You two are practically inseparable."

"Would you believe me if I told you that I got arrested?"

"Are you serious?"

Colt told her everything that had happened over the last few days, and when he was done, she started to say something, but then she stopped. The long stretch of silence made him nervous. "I don't even know what to say," she finally said. "I mean, the whole thing is insane."

"Tell me about it."

She took a deep breath, like an actress composing herself before she went onstage. "Okay, do you have the flash drive?"

"It's right here." He reached into his pocket and held it up to the camera.

"I want you to send me the files—all of them—but make sure you use your phone, not your laptop. Your line isn't secure."

"Okay, but . . ." Colt averted his eyes.

"But what?"

"I don't know," he said, trying to avoid relaying the thoughts that were dancing around in his head. "Do you think Oz will see them?"

"Why? It's not like he's in on it."

Colt didn't respond.

"Wait, you think he is?"

"I don't know," Colt said. "I mean, I hope not, but . . ." He explained his theory, and when he was done, she just sat there and scratched her dog behind the ears.

"How many times could Oz have killed you since the two of you started hanging out?" she finally asked.

"I hadn't thought about that."

"Don't get me wrong," she said. "I mean, I'm not saying that he's *not* a part of some conspiracy to kill you, but one way or the other, we need to find out."

"How?"

She shrugged. "We'll figure something out. Look, I have to finish packing or I'm going to be up all night. Don't forget to send me those files, okay?"

"Yeah, sure."

"Don't worry, it'll all work out. Just make sure you act normal around him, or he's going to think that something is up."

Colt had no idea how he was supposed to act normal when it seemed his best friend wanted to kill him.

:: CHAPTER 23 ::

Colt woke up to the sound of pots and pans clanging in the kitchen as Grandpa made breakfast. He opened one eye and groaned. It was still dark outside, and he wanted to go back to sleep, but it was his last morning in Arizona and he still hadn't finished packing.

His tired fingers probed through the laundry in search of the alarm clock that had fallen off his nightstand, but he didn't have much luck. His shoulder was stiff, and he was about to give up when he felt something cold and metallic beneath a damp towel. The tin clock was still ticking despite the abuse, and according to the hands, it was barely six o'clock.

Outside, a garbage truck rumbled down the street, its brakes screeching at every stop. As usual, the neighbor's dog started barking, and Colt figured he might as well get up. He rolled out of bed just as the truck pulled up to the curb in front of Grandpa's lawn, the vibrations from the engine shaking the window. "Great," he said as he knocked over a cardboard box, dumping at least a hundred comic books across the hardwood floor. He thought about picking them up, but decided to add that to his list of everything else he had to do.

"You're up early," Grandpa said as he flipped a pancake on the griddle. He was still in his pajamas and some old slippers that were cracked and faded with age. "Care for some breakfast?"

"Sure," Colt attempted to say, but it came out as some kind of grunt. It was all he could do to keep his eyes open, and he slumped into one of the chairs wondering if he had the energy to stand back up and pour himself a cup of coffee.

From the look of things, Grandpa had been awake long enough to read the morning paper. It was folded neatly next to his reading glasses and the television remote. Colt started to reach for the sports section, but he stopped when he saw the lead article on the front page. The headline read FREEWAY GUNMEN TAKEN INTO CUSTODY.

He sat up straight and read the story once, and then again. According to the report, two men were arrested in connection with the shootings on the Loop 202 Santan Freeway. Local police received several anonymous tips that led them to a rental property on a private golf course. When they raided the home they found over fifty pounds of marijuana, EMP grenades, a plasma rifle, and an armored Mercedes sedan with bulletproof windows and a pair of M60 machine guns mounted on the hood.

Colt sat slack-jawed, staring at the mug shots of the suspects. One of the men was older, probably in his sixties, with a thick shock of white hair and heavy eyebrows. The other looked barely old enough to have a driver's license. His hair was long in the front, but shorter in the back, and he was scowling at the camera.

"Did you see this?" Colt asked, though he already knew the answer. Grandpa was the only person Colt knew who read the newspaper from front to back, though for some reason he always started with the obituaries.

Grandpa looked over his shoulder. "Are you talking about the shootings?" he asked, scooping some scrambled eggs onto a plate. "Nice bit of police work, wouldn't you say?"

Colt frowned, wondering if Grandpa was serious. "Yeah, except the part where they arrested the wrong people," he said, not bothering to mask his sarcasm. If someone squinted and looked at the pictures from a distance, the suspects looked a little like Colt and Grandpa, but the arrests were a fraud. "They didn't have anything to do with it. I mean, what if they have families or—"

"Those men are wanted felons," Grandpa said. His voice was calm and his face impassive. "The older one? He's ex-mafia from New Jersey and a convicted felon who admitted to murdering more than a dozen people. In exchange for his testimony against a crime boss, the FBI dropped all charges and sent him to Arizona as part of the witness protection program. But instead of living a nice quiet life, he decided to get involved in drug trafficking. And most of the product that he brings into the country ends up with people your age, and sometimes younger."

He set a plate of pancakes, scrambled eggs with cheddar cheese, and crisp bacon in front of Colt, then went back to serve himself. "The other guy shot and killed a woman during a robbery attempt last week. He was a junkie, and he was looking for money to get his next fix. Luckily her three children were at Grandma's house, because in his state of mind, he wouldn't have cared who he shot. So I don't think you need to feel sorry for either one of them."

"But I don't get it," Colt said, trying to work everything out in his head. "How did they get arrested for what happened last night? And where did they get EMP grenades, let alone an armored car with machine guns mounted on the hood? It's not like you can buy that stuff at a sporting goods store."

"You'd be surprised." Grandpa sat down across from Colt and slathered butter on his pancakes before drowning them in maple syrup. "Look, I don't know the particulars, and to tell you the truth, I don't want to know," he said, taking a bite. A drop of syrup ran down his chin. "The truth of the matter is that there are entities with enough power to bend reality so long as it suits their needs—and it's not just the good guys either."

"Is that what you were doing on the phone last night?" Colt asked. It was hard to believe that Grandpa had the kind of connections that could make something like that happen.

"I explained our situation to a friend and let him decide how to handle it," Grandpa said between bites. "Now eat your breakfast before it gets cold."

Colt bit into a strip of bacon, but his eyes kept drifting to the pictures of the men in the newspaper. Maybe they were criminals, and from the sound of things, they deserved to go to prison for a very long time. But knowing that someone had enough power to plant evidence, falsify witnesses, and get the media to buy into all of it was terrifying. He wondered how many people were rotting away behind bars, framed for crimes they didn't commit. He wondered if it could ever happen to him.

When they were finished eating, Grandpa cleared their plates and filled the sink with warm water and dish soap. "I know you have a lot going on in that head of yours," he said as he ran a sponge over the spatula. "You're a lot like your mother in that way. Once she got her mind locked on an idea, it was hard for her to let go. But what's done is done, and those men were heading to prison one way or the other. Besides, you have bigger concerns right now."

"You mean Lobo?" Colt swirled the remnants of his orange juice in the bottom of his glass.

"I mean that disaster you call a bedroom." Grandpa smiled, though it was faint. "Look, things are going to get more complicated over the next few weeks, and I wish more than anything that I could take your place, but all the wishing in the world isn't going to change a thing." He wiped his hands on a dishtowel. "Like it or not, there isn't much more I can do—not at this age. But there are people in place who will help you—people you can trust."

"Like who?" Colt almost laughed. The idea of trusting anyone seemed ludicrous at best. If anything, he'd never felt more alienated in his life. His grandfather knew that the government had shot him up with alien blood, and it was starting to look like his best friend was aware of a plot to kill him. But neither one had said a word.

"For starters, the DAA is investigating Operation Nemesis," he said. "The rest will show themselves when the time is right." Grandpa walked over to one of the cabinets and pulled out a wooden box. "Look, I know things have been a bit strained between us. This isn't much, but I wanted to give it to you before you left."

The box was small, and its edges were worn from age. Colt ran his fingers over the smooth surface and found two brass hinges and a single clasp, which he opened with his thumb. The inside of the box was lined with felt, and he reached inside to pull out a piece of crumbled tissue paper that held a medallion strung to a ball chain necklace. The medallion was a copper color, like a tarnished penny, with a cross on one side and a verse on the other: *God is our refuge and strength, a very present help in trouble. Ps. 46:1*

"I wore that when I was in the service," Grandpa said, his eyes distant as though he was recalling a lost memory. "You know, I've always thought it was funny how we glorify war in movies and television . . . and now we have those video games where you shoot to kill your enemy." He shook his head. "There's nothing glorious about war . . . men shot, their bodies mangled as they call out for their mothers. And there's not a darned thing you can do for any of them, other than maybe give them a packet of morphine and hope they go fast." He took out a handkerchief and wiped his nose. "The only way I got through it without losing my mind was this medallion. I wasn't worried about survival . . . none of us were. We all thought that we were going home in a pine box. But I'd rub that thing between my thumb and forefinger and pray that the Good Lord would give me the strength to finish my mission."

Colt held the medallion in his palm, and he could see a worn path where his grandfather had rubbed across the surface. "Thanks," he said as he slipped it over his neck.

"I want you to know I'm proud of you," Grandpa said. His voice was shaky as he walked over to finish the dishes.

Colt just sat there, his eyes fixed on what was left of his orange juice as he rubbed the medallion and prayed for strength.

After a long, hot shower, he got dressed and went to work packing the rest of his things. Other than some toiletries and a change of clothes, he wasn't supposed to bring anything to Virginia. That meant his comic book collection had to stay behind, along with the action figures and his dad's Phantom Flyer signet ring.

He wrapped frames in towels, stopping to look at each picture as memories of his parents came flooding back. His favorite was a picture where the three of them were at Sea World after the

Shamu show. He was maybe six or seven, and somehow he had talked them into sitting in the splash zone. He remembered how his mom howled as the wall of water crashed over her. Before long they were all drenched from head to toe, smiling and laughing under the warm summer sun.

Soon, just about everything he owned was in cardboard boxes, and each time he sealed one shut it felt like he was burying a part of his past. He stacked them neatly against the wall and pulled his sheets off the bed, but when he went to put them in the washing machine, his phone beeped. It was an e-mail from Danielle.

She had stayed up half the night going through the files from Operation Nemesis. Colt was definitely on the same hit list that included Senator Bishop, along with a member of the CIA, a federal judge, and another senator from Massachusetts—the one who died from a heart attack while she was jogging last fall.

According to the documents, the deaths were either accidental or the person died from natural causes. One was lost at sea after a boating incident, another drowned during a triathlon. There was a car wreck, a suicide, and someone lost a long battle against cancer. But there was no pattern, and none of them had been shot, stabbed, or dropped from the top of a building. Then again, as Colt had found out that morning, reports could be falsified if a person had the right connections . . . and there was no doubt that Lobo had connections.

:: CHAPTER 24 ::

Grandpa got a call just as they were leaving for the airport. Apparently an investigative team from the Department of Alien Affairs found traces of ozone and other particulates specific to portal travel near the motorcycle used in last night's attack.

They kept that stretch of freeway shut down all night and into the day, making the morning commute into downtown Phoenix a nightmare. But they couldn't risk losing a potential lead, even if it was just a footprint, bloodstain, or even a broken fingernail. Search units scoured a ten-mile radius through the desert and into neighborhoods using equipment that was decades beyond what local crime scene investigators used or even knew existed. They still didn't find anything.

"Where do you think he is?" Colt asked, trying not to sound anxious.

"Probably in a hole somewhere licking his wounds," Grandpa said. "But don't worry, he'll be back."

Grandpa decided to take Colt to the airport in the pickup, just in case someone noticed the Cadillac and called the police.

He didn't say much of anything during the drive, not that he had ever been much of a talker. But he seemed distracted.

"What's wrong?" Colt asked as they wound around the airport, skirting the terminals until they came to an airstrip reserved for private jets.

"I was just thinking about the day I dropped your father off at the academy," Grandpa said, turning down a short drive that led to a chain link gate. Two men stood in front, each dressed in military fatigues and holding an M4 carbine assault rifle. Grandpa didn't bother to open his window. He simply held up the CHAOS badge that he still carried in his wallet, and they let him through.

"I thought he'd be nervous. After all, he'd never been gone from home for more than a week or two at summer camp. But when I drove up to the building, he shook my hand, opened the door, and marched right up those steps without looking back.

"I don't think your grandmother talked to me for a week," he said with a chuckle. "She was furious, not that I could blame her. She knew the sacrifices involved with serving your country, and CHAOS is no different. I think she was hoping he would go to medical school, or become a shoe salesman—it didn't matter, as long as he wasn't a soldier. But when Roger got that invitation, there was no changing his mind. He was going to save the world and that's all there was to it."

"Are you sure I wasn't adopted?" Colt asked as he watched one of the jets race down the runway. The nose lifted into the air, and a moment later it was little more than a speck on the horizon. "I mean, I don't mind serving my country, but I just got my driver's license and . . . well . . . I don't know. It's just that so much has happened over these last few months that I was kind of hoping I could stay here awhile longer."

Grandpa turned to him and smiled. "I was hoping that myself," he said. "But you're going to do just fine. And besides, we'll see each other soon enough." He pulled into a parking spot next to Danielle's parents, who were removing her luggage from the trunk of their car. Colt sat there, knowing that the moment he opened the door his life was going to change forever.

"By the way," Grandpa said, "you were right. I should have told you about the tests."

"It's okay," Colt said. "I probably would have done the same thing if I were you."

Grandpa pulled on the emergency brake and stepped out of the cab to great the Salazars. Danielle's father shook his hand, and her mom wrapped her arms around his neck. Grandpa held her close, patting her on the back as tears ran down her cheeks.

"Why do they have to be so dramatic?" Danielle asked, trying to sound exasperated despite her own red eyes and puffy cheeks.

"You're right," he said. "I mean, it's not like they're sending their teenaged daughter away to save the world from an alien horde or anything."

"Whatever."

Colt grabbed his duffel bag from the back of the truck. "I thought we were supposed to travel light," he said when he saw Danielle's luggage.

"This is traveling light." She was standing next to two large roller suitcases and an oversized toiletry bag, not to mention her purse and the backpack that held her laptop.

Across the tarmac, two men in dark suits stood next to a charcoal-colored jet with a white CHAOS logo painted on the side. Colt thought that it looked like a shark, with a pointed nose and wings that jetted from the back like pectoral fins.

"I've never ridden in a private jet before," Danielle said. "This is gonna be fun."

Colt shrugged. His dad had owned a charter company that catered to athletes, movie stars, and wealthy businessmen, and every once in a while he'd take Colt on a fishing trip to Seattle, or they'd fly to visit one of his brothers.

"Sorry. I forgot that you're used to traveling like a rock star," Danielle said.

"It's not that."

"I know." She walked over so nobody could overhear the conversation. "Look, if you mope around, Oz is going to know that something is up. So you have to act normal, okay?"

"What am I supposed to do?"

"Fake it," she said. "And it probably wouldn't hurt to sleep with one eye open until we know if he's involved."

"Funny."

A few minutes later a black SUV with tinted windows pulled up next to Grandpa's truck. The driver was Asian, with a shaved head and broad shoulders, and when he opened the door, Colt could see that his jacket had a CHAOS badge on the sleeve.

Oz jumped out of the backseat, a broad grin on his face as he tossed his enormous duffel bag next to Danielle's luggage. "Who's ready to bash some alien skulls?"

"Remember," Danielle whispered to Colt. "Act normal."

One of the pilots took Colt's duffel bag and placed it next to Danielle's luggage in one of the cargo bays. She ran over to say good-bye to her parents one last time, hugging each of them before she ran up the stairs and into the jet.

Grandpa stood there, his hands in his pockets as a strong

breeze tousled his silver hair. "I'll see you in a few weeks," he said with a nod.

Colt felt lost and desperate, like a bird being forced from the nest before it could fly. Without realizing it, he reached for the medallion that hung around his neck.

"Wait until you see what I brought for the flight," Oz said as he wrapped his massive arm around Colt's shoulder. "It's going to blow your mind."

:: CHAPTER 25 ::

The exterior of the jet was the model of military efficiency, with sleek lines and a titanium airframe that protected against high temperatures caused by traveling at supersonic speed. Inside, it dripped with luxury. The jet was surprisingly spacious, with oversized leather recliners. Each had a monitor mounted to the ceiling, along with a small table that retracted into the wall in case any of the passengers wanted to use the footrest.

Danielle was already sitting down, her eyes hidden behind sunglasses as she stared out the window to where her parents stood with Grandpa. She was wearing earbuds, and the music was loud enough that Colt could hear it from where he was standing.

"Can you believe it?" Oz said, taking the seat across the aisle from her. His knee was bouncing up and down, and his eyes were lit with anticipation. "By this time tomorrow, we're going to be actual CHAOS agents."

"You mean cadets," Danielle said. She pulled the earbuds out. "We have to graduate from the academy first, and even then we still need to finish college before they'll consider our applications."

"Don't be a downer, Salazar."

"What? It's true."

Colt walked to the back of the cabin, checking every nook and cranny to see if Krone had somehow found his way onto the jet. He looked in the bathroom and underneath the conference table. He even checked in the fridge behind the bar, but all he found were soda, energy drinks, and bottled waters.

"Is it okay if I take one of these?" he asked, reaching for a root beer.

"That's why they're there," Oz said. "Grab me one too, will you?"

The pilot asked them to fasten their seat belts, and a few minutes later they were in the air. If the weather cooperated, they would reach Washington, DC, in a little over four hours. Danielle, who still hadn't removed her sunglasses, sat there with her head against the window, sniffling as she watched the world disappear behind a bank of clouds.

Colt tried to be discreet as he pulled up a picture of Lily on his phone. She was standing on top of Camelback Mountain as the sun set over the city. She hadn't wanted him to take it, because she was sweaty and she wasn't wearing any makeup, but Colt loved that picture. After their hike, they'd gone back to her house and he'd sat on the porch swing while she played her guitar.

He closed the image and sat back in his seat, lamenting the way things had ended between them. Like a jerk, he'd never called her to apologize, and now it was too late. He doubted that she would take his call even if he tried.

He was just starting to nod off when Oz tapped him on the shoulder.

"Okay, so check this out," Oz said as he unzipped his backpack. "I figured that we were going to need something to do, so I stopped by Greg's Comics."

"We left a half-hour late because you went to a comic book shop?" Danielle said. "You're impossible."

"Thank you," Oz said. "Anyway, Howard—you know, the guy who runs the shop—he was at an estate sale last week and he picked up the complete run of *Phantom Flyer and the Agents of Chaos.*"

"No way," Colt said, sliding to the edge of his chair so he could get a better look. "How much?"

Oz shrugged. "He gave me a good deal. You know, as a kind of going-away present. Anyway, some of the issues are in rough shape, but I got them to read, not to sit in Mylar bags and collect dust for fifty years." He pulled out a thick stack and handed them to Colt, who forgot all about assassination plots as he flipped through them, drinking in every glorious detail.

There was one called *Attack of the Gray Aliens*, where flying saucers flew as part of the Luftwaffe during the Blitz over London. Other covers showed images of wolf men with Nazi armbands and robots with *SS* emblazoned on their metallic chests; one even showed the Phantom Flyer standing over Dracula's coffin holding a wooden stake and a mallet. Colt wondered how much of the stories was true. After all, the comics were supposed to be loosely based on actual events that took place. Did that mean vampires were real?

"This is beyond incredible," Colt said as he gently pulled one of the comics out of its protective bag. The corners were a bit rough, and the color had started to fade, but other than that it was in prime condition. As he cracked it open, he closed his eyes and drank in the musty aroma of the newsprint like it was a fragrant bouquet of flowers.

"You realize that you're smelling a comic book, right?"

Danielle asked. She had removed her sunglasses now that her eyes were dry.

"Don't knock it," Oz said. He tried to get her to sniff one of the books, but she squirmed away and pinned herself against the window with her arms covering her face.

"I'll pass!"

"Do you think they'll make comic books about our adventures one day?" Oz asked as he sat back in his chair.

"Maybe," Colt said, sounding disinterested. Danielle gave him one of those looks where he knew he had said the wrong thing, so he tried again. "I mean, if the Thule actually attack and we manage to survive, then sure. Why not?"

"I wonder what we should call it," Oz said, scratching his chin as he looked at the ceiling. "How about *The Amazing Adventures of Oz and Colt*?"

"Aren't you forgetting someone?" Danielle asked.

"Sorry," Oz said. "And their faithful sidekick, Danielle."

"I don't think so."

As they quibbled about the title, Colt turned his attention to the sky, which had turned a strange shade of gray that bordered on purple. It reminded him of the summer storms back in Iowa where his mom had grown up. The clouds were thick, and rolling thunder followed a brilliant flash of lightning.

The intercom crackled as the captain's voice echoed through the cabin. "As you can see, we're experiencing a little unexpected weather. We're going to climb to about 38,000 feet to see if we can't find some clear skies."

The jagged afterglow of lightning hung in the horizon as the thunder boomed. There was something in the clouds. It was only a silhouette, but whatever it was, it was enormous.

"Did you guys see that?" Colt asked.

"See what?" Oz asked, leaning over so he could look out the window.

"I don't know," Colt said. "Maybe I was just hallucinating." He lay back against the headrest as another burst of lightning filled the sky.

Danielle's eyes went wide. Then she screamed.

There was no way that something like that could exist, yet there it was, not more than a kilometer or two away. The creature looked something like a jellyfish, although it was as big as a three-bedroom house. Its membrane was translucent, revealing a strange network of nerves that looked like a cluster of wires. Bursts of light flashed across the complex trails, firing in rapid succession.

Colt watched dozens of tentacles undulate below its membrane like water snakes skimming the surface of a pond. "What is that thing?"

"I don't know," Oz said. "Maybe it escaped from one of the CHAOS facilities in New Mexico."

Colt wondered what kind of facility was big enough to hold something like that. Was it in a warehouse? Some kind of bunker deep underground? And if there was a place that housed giant flying jellyfish, what other kinds of creatures were locked up there?

Oz pulled out his phone and took a few pictures.

"What are you doing?"

"I want to put them on my Facebook page."

"Are you serious?"

"No," Oz said as he took another picture. "I'm going to send them to someone at CHAOS so we can find out what it is."

There was a flash of light followed by a loud clang. It sounded like somebody was pounding on the hull with a sledgehammer. The cabin started to shake, and the jet dropped. A tentacle slapped Colt's window and made a sick noise, like rotting meat thrown against a hard surface. He scrambled to get out of his seat, forgetting that he was buckled in as something like suction cups latched on to the glass, leaving an oily residue.

Danielle screamed, her fingers digging in the armrests as her eyes scanned the ceiling. A sound like metal being ripped apart echoed through the cabin as the monster latched on. It beat the glass, and Colt watched as his window started to splinter. Veins appeared like a spiderweb as they spread across the surface.

"That thing isn't alone," Oz said. The sky was filled with the strange monsters floating through the storm like a school of jellyfish while winds sent waves across their membranes.

The overhead lights flickered as the ceiling bowed. Colt didn't know if the aircraft was right side up or upside down as the intercom crackled to life.

"If we can break free from this thing, there's a soft spot in the atmosphere," the captain said. "I've called our coordinates in, and if we time it right we should be able to make a jump."

"Wait," Colt said. "As in a gateway?"

Random gateways weren't exactly stable. They were there one second and gone the next, and even if they found one before it closed, there was no way to know where it led. Then again, if the only alternative was sitting there while a giant flying jellyfish ripped the jet apart, they didn't have much of a choice.

There was an explosion followed by a burst of light. White streaks ran across the hull and down the wings, crackling and swirling as they went. The creature let out a piercing cry, and the fiery current engulfed its tentacles. A moment later the jet was free. The pilot banked hard to the right, and as the plane wove through the field of hungry tentacles, Colt hoped the aircraft would hold together long enough to make the jump. He craned his neck and spotted the dark patch of sky. It was black against the deep gray, and clouds swirled like a living frame as lightning rippled across the surface.

The jet shot forward, veering toward the gateway as the cabin shook and engines roared. But just when Colt thought they were free, a tentacle lashed out, hitting one of the wings. The jet dipped hard to the right, and his head smashed against the window. He blinked, trying to gather his thoughts as more tentacles wrapped around the aircraft, crushing the hull until the ceiling started to cave in.

A second jellyfish moved toward them, its tentacles dancing with abandon. Colt closed his eyes, but at the last possible moment the pilot thrust the engines to full power and the jet went into a barrel roll. Somehow the pilot managed to break free from the writhing tentacles and into open airspace before the nose of the jet broke the surface of the portal.

:: CHAPTER 26 ::

The gateway wasn't as random as they had thought. The soft spot in the atmosphere might have become a portal given time, but it needed some coaxing if they wanted to use it to escape from the jellyfish monsters.

After the pilot relayed their coordinates, a team in Nevada programmed the gateway using experimental technology that was similar to a personal teleporting device, but on a much larger scale. The machine was in development to use for military troop transport, allowing instantaneous travel instead of relying on ships and airplanes. Up to that point, no human had been used in any of the trials, only robots and drones. If the calculations were off—even by a fraction—the gateway would close, trapping any-one and anything inside. But Lobo had given the order himself, and thankfully the gateway worked.

The mangled jet made it to Ronald Reagan Washington National Airport, where the pilot landed on a private airstrip far from the commercial terminals. No sooner had the door opened than Colt grabbed Danielle's hand and headed down the narrow stairs and onto the tarmac, where a fleet of emergency vehicles waited.

"I'm never flying again," Danielle said as the wind blew strands of hair into her face.

Though it was the middle of the afternoon, it was already getting dark. The sky was overcast, and tiny white flakes fell from thick clouds, though they melted as soon as they hit the ground. It was just enough to make everything wet and miserable. Colt zipped his jacket and stuffed his hands in his pockets as a paramedic rushed over with a blanket, offering to wrap it around his shoulders. "I'm okay," he said, waving her off.

"Where's Oz?" Danielle asked. "I thought he was right behind us."

As Colt scanned the crowd, he noticed the CHAOS agents. There were at least a dozen, maybe more. Some wore suits with long trench coats and others had dark jackets with CHAOS written across the back in bold yellow letters. All were armed, and Colt felt trapped. If Lobo told them that Colt was a Russian spy or that he'd been recruited into a fringe terrorist cell, there was a good chance they would shoot first and ask questions later.

"There he is," Danielle said, pointing to where Oz stood in front of a black Mercedes R350 Crossover. It seemed like an extravagant vehicle, considering organizations like the FBI typically drove Chevy Suburbans. Maybe, Colt thought, lavish spending was part of the reason that Senator Bishop and other members of the oversight committee wanted to oust Lobo as the director.

Oz was locked in a conversation with a tall alien who was extraordinarily thin. She had pointed ears and something that looked like a cross between a dorsal fin and a Mohawk running down the center of her head. Her skin was a shade that reminded Colt of sea foam, her eyes were enormous, and instead of lips and a nose she had some kind of beak that made her look like a bald parrot.

As Colt and Danielle made their way across the tarmac, Oz's eyes kept darting about. He was standing close enough to the alien that he didn't need to talk in much more than a whisper, so Colt wasn't able to overhear any of their conversation. When Oz saw them approaching, he nodded and the alien turned around.

"What's that all about?" Danielle asked.

"I'm not sure," Colt said. Watching the exchange left him with a pit in his stomach, and that wasn't a good sign.

There was a flurry of motion, and Colt turned to see Ms. Skoglund bustling through the crowd in a thick coat, with fluffy white earmuffs and a matching scarf, mittens, and boots. "Oh my, are you two okay?" she asked, her face flush with concern.

"Yeah, we're fine," Colt said, confused.

"When they told us what happened up there, I was sick with worry."

"Don't take this the wrong way or anything, but what are you doing here?" Colt asked as Ms. Skoglund enveloped him in an enormous embrace.

"You're looking at the newly appointed head of online security for the entire CHAOS Military Academy," she said, her face beaming with pride.

"That's amazing," Danielle said.

"I know, right? It's like we're all one big flock migrating out here together. And I even get to teach a couple of classes. Can you believe it? Me, a teacher?" She turned and coughed, covering her mouth with her fluffy mitten. "Anyway, I'm also here as your official greeter and chauffeur, so what do you say we pile into the van and head over to the academy?"

"What about Oz?" Danielle asked.

Ms. Skoglund shrugged. "He wasn't on my list."

:: CHAPTER 27 ::

The CHAOS Academy was less than twenty miles away from the airport, but thanks to the D.C. traffic it was going to take an hour or more to get there. Ms. Skoglund used the time to catch them up on what she knew about Operation Nemesis, which admittedly wasn't much. She had just flown in that morning, and she'd spent most of the day on the telephone trying to find the luggage that the airline had lost. Spying on Lobo would have to wait until the morning.

She didn't seem concerned that Oz had been assigned to another driver. After all, there were something like two hundred students flying in throughout the day, and she had spent most of it shuttling back and forth between the airport and the academy.

"Who was Oz talking with?" Danielle asked.

"I think her name is Giru Ba, but don't quote me on that," Ms. Skoglund said. "I haven't been officially introduced, but I was told she's one of the instructors at the flight school."

Colt shut his eyes, pretending to sleep as Danielle told Ms. Skoglund all about the flying jellyfish and how she was convinced they were all going to die. "But I just realized something," she said as she sat up straight, her eyes wide. "When that thing latched on to the plane, it was trying to break through Colt's window—like it knew who he was."

Ms. Skoglund looked at Colt through the rearview mirror. "Is that true?"

"I doubt it," he said, shrugging.

"Think about it," Danielle said. "It's like that viper wasp back in Arizona. It pretty much ignored us and went after you."

"That's crazy."

"It makes perfect sense. Trident created a biochip that allowed them to turn average people into remote control assassins, right? So why wouldn't it work on animals?"

Ms. Skoglund bit the inside of her cheek. "I think Danielle might be onto something."

"Why would Lobo send those things after me if Oz was in the jet?" Colt asked. "Do you think he'd be willing to kill his own son just to get to me?"

"What are the odds of getting attacked by an alien?" Danielle asked.

"CHAOS has confirmed about four hundred attacks since January," Ms. Skoglund said. "And there are something like seven billion people on the planet."

"Give me a second," Danielle said as she entered the numbers into an app on her phone. "There. That puts your odds at 1 in 17,500,000. But somehow you managed to get attacked twice in the same week. And that doesn't strike you as peculiar?"

"Maybe," Colt said as he leaned back against the headrest. "But it doesn't explain why Lobo would send those things after me if he knew that Oz was there."

"Okay," Ms. Skoglund said. "I want you to be casual about

this, but tell me if you recognize the guy driving the Mercedes. He's about three cars behind us, and he's wearing a black turtleneck and round glasses."

Colt turned around, pretending he was checking on the luggage. He could see the car that Ms. Skoglund was talking about. It was a black CL550 Coupe, but he didn't recognize the driver. "Never seen him before."

"Me either," Danielle said.

"Nuts," Ms. Skoglund said. "He looks so familiar."

"You don't think he's tailing us, do you?" Danielle asked.

"Can you see his front license plate?"

Danielle nodded. "I think so. It looks like it's from Virginia."

"See if you can find out whose name the car is registered under. Can you do that?"

"I'll have it for you in less than a minute," Danielle said as she plugged the number into her phone.

"That's my girl," Ms. Skoglund said as she put her blinker on and eased into the right lane. "Now let's see if he takes the bait." Sure enough, he followed her. "All right, once is a coincidence, but twice is a fact." This time she put the left blinker on before she crossed the median back to the center lane.

Colt couldn't have been more obvious as he turned around to watch out the back window. The snow was falling more heavily, limiting visibility, but he could still see the Mercedes as it cut into the center lane.

"He's totally following us," Ms. Skoglund said, sounding almost excited.

"You're not going to believe this," Danielle said. "The car is registered to Aldrich Koenig."

"As in the shape-shifting, six-armed alien who used to run

Trident Biotech?" Colt asked. "Isn't he supposed to be locked up in an underground facility somewhere in the middle of the desert?"

"A little on the dramatic side, but yeah," Danielle said.

"The guy driving that car doesn't look anything like him."

"As you said, he's a shapeshifter. He can look like whoever he wants," Danielle said. "Besides, just because the car is registered under his name, it doesn't mean that he's the one driving it. It could be his butler, or a friend, or anybody."

"Or Krone," Colt said.

"You have a camera on that phone, right?" Ms. Skoglund asked.

"Of course," Danielle said.

"Give it to old blue eyes back there so he can take a picture of the guy, and then I think we'll ditch him."

Colt snapped the picture as the Mercedes tore into the far left lane, cutting off a tow truck. The driver of the truck slammed on the brakes, and the back end started to swerve. He spun the steering wheel, trying to regain control, but the highway was slick from the snow. The truck flipped over, rolling at least seven times before Colt lost track. Tires screeched and horns blared as everyone tried to get out of the way.

"Hold tight," Ms. Skoglund said. "Things are about to get interesting." She started weaving in and out of traffic with the abandon of a New York City taxi driver. The van cut across two lanes, narrowly avoiding a collision with a school bus before she swerved back the other way.

"He's right behind us," Colt said as he watched the Mercedes through the rear window. It looked like the driver was reaching over to grab something out of the glove compartment. "Please don't be a gun."

"Get down!" Ms. Skoglund shouted.

The driver rolled down his window and fired three shots from a Walther P99 with tactical lights and a suppressor kit, each exploding from the barrel with a flash. The first missed, ricocheting off a road sign. The second hit the asphalt, but the third caught Ms. Skoglund's mirror. The glass shattered and she screamed as she took her hands off the wheel. The van cut hard to the right, barreling across the traffic and onto the shoulder. She slammed on the brakes and the van teetered, going on two wheels before it touched back down. "All right," she said, sounding out of breath. "Time to end this."

"Wait . . . are you going to shoot him?" Danielle asked.

"As much as I'd like to, I'm going to have to improvise," she said. "They won't give me a gun." She pressed the gas pedal to the floor and cut into the center lane. "Come on," she said, watching the Mercedes through the rearview mirror. "You know you want me."

It sped up until it was even with their van. The driver leveled the barrel of his Walther P99 at Ms. Skoglund, but she just smiled. "Got you!" She slammed the brakes and cranked the wheel to the left, clipping the back end of the Mercedes with her front bumper.

The sedan fishtailed and smashed into a pickup truck with oversized tires. The truck ran over the hood of the Mercedes before barreling across the median and into oncoming traffic. The Mercedes flipped over before skidding across the parkway, sparks flying as metal ground against asphalt.

Ms. Skoglund exited the George Washington Memorial Parkway and took back roads the rest of the way, hoping to avoid local law enforcement. Colt didn't mind the diversion. The Virginia countryside was beautiful, filled with rolling hills and thick trees, though most had lost their fall colors.

"This is it." Ms. Skoglund pulled the van onto a nondescript road that cut through what looked like a forest. "If either of you wants to make a run for it, now's your chance. Because once we're inside the gates, there's no turning back. Your lives are going to become the property of the Central Headquarters Against the Occult and Supernatural for the next eighteen months. After that it only gets worse."

Danielle looked at Colt through the rearview mirror. "Worse than sitting through another one of Mr. Pfeffer's lectures in world history? I don't think so."

They laughed as they followed the winding road for about a mile before they came to an iron gate topped with spikes. Ms. Skoglund held up what she called an identicard—it looked a bit like the school ID they carried at Chandler High, only it was programmed with data like blood type, allergies, and level of security clearance.

The gate opened, and she drove up to a building that wasn't anything like what Colt had expected. There was no grassy lawn, towering pillars, or ivy creeping up the front of the façade. There wasn't even a flagpole. Nothing about this place screamed private school for the elite, but maybe that whole brick mansion thing was just in the movies.

"This is the CHAOS Academy?" Danielle asked, clearly as shocked as he was. She still hadn't unbuckled her seat belt, as though by doing so she would be committing to something that she wasn't quite ready for. "It's kind of . . . I don't know. I guess it's not what I expected."

"Yeah, it has that whole psychiatric hospital vibe, but don't worry. They keep all the crazies locked up in the basement."

Danielle looked at her, eyes wide and jaw hanging slightly open.

"It was a joke," Ms. Skoglund said, patting her on the back of the hand. "Trust me, this place may not have much in the way of curb appeal, but inside it's amazing—especially for a tech head like you."

"Okay," Danielle said, her voice weak.

Colt wasn't used to seeing her like this. Growing up, she hadn't been afraid of anything. He remembered the time when they were seven and her mom saw a scorpion on their kitchen tile. Colt was ready to climb up on the countertop, but Danielle trapped it beneath a glass bowl until the pest control team showed up.

"Don't worry, you'll be fine," Ms. Skoglund said. "I'll see you at orientation tonight and try to sneak you into the computer lab for a private tour."

Danielle tried to force a smile as her hand found the release for her seat belt.

"You better get going," Ms. Skoglund said. "I'm supposed to pick up some of the other recruits in a half hour, and I still need to figure out how I'm going to explain what happened to the van."

Colt slid his door open and stepped onto the sidewalk as a cold breeze burst across the school grounds. He waited as Danielle sat there an extra moment longer, then she joined him. "What about our luggage?"

"You'll get it soon enough." Ms. Skoglund reached over, stretching her short arm as far as it could reach to shut Danielle's door. The lock clicked and she drove off, leaving them standing alone in the cold.

:: CHAPTER 28 ::

There was a set of double doors at the top of the stairs, but the glass was tinted so they couldn't see inside. Colt looked for a doorbell or some kind of buzzer, but he couldn't find anything.

"Just knock," Danielle said, but before he could raise his hand there was a buzzing sound and one of the doors clicked open.

They walked into a foyer that was at least the size of the gymnasium back at Chandler High. The floor was covered in marble tiles, and the glass panes along the ceiling were streaked with condensation from the snow. There was no art on the walls or even an exit sign over the doors. In fact, there was no decor at all. It was sterile. Lifeless. Intimidating.

On the opposite end of the room was a reception area where a soldier stood in full combat uniform. He wore a ballistic vest and had a M4 Carbine that hung from a strap slung over his shoulder. The tag embroidered on his chest read *Hayden*.

"Um, hi," Colt said. "We were wondering if this is where we're supposed to go . . . you know, for the CHAOS Academy?"

"Names, please." Hayden's voice was rich and dark like his skin.

"I'm Colt McAlister, and this is—"

"I know my own name," Danielle whispered. She threw her shoulders back and stared the man straight in the eye. "I'm Danielle Selena Salazar. Do you need to see my invitation?"

"That won't be necessary," he said. "Stand by for full body scan."

"Excuse me?" Danielle asked.

"Initiate sequence 3-5-Alpha."

Two metal spheres rose from behind the counter, each about the size of a bowling ball. Somehow they flew across the room until one hovered over Colt's head and the other was directly above Danielle. Apertures opened, bathing them in green light. A moment later they were looking at holographic replicas of themselves. They were green and slightly translucent, like an x-ray. And they were spot on.

"What's that hanging around your neck?" Hayden asked.

"It's just something my grandpa gave me," Colt said, fingering the tarnished surface. "He wore it when he fought in World War II."

"So it's true?" Hayden asked, his face stern and his voice measured. "Murdoch McAlister is your grandfather?"

"Yes, sir," Colt said.

Hayden smiled. "You've been the only thing people around here have been talking about for weeks."

Colt wasn't sure how to respond.

"Me and the fellas, we were impressed with what you did at Trident. You really went toe-to-toe with one of them lizards?"

"It's not like I knew what I was doing," Colt said. "I just got lucky."

"Ain't no such thing as luck," Hayden said. "But you know that already, don't you?" He started to say something else, but he must have thought better of it. "Now, are either of you carrying a cell phone, camera, or any other type of recording device?"

"I left mine in the van," Colt said.

"My phone is in my purse, but—"

"I'm afraid you'll have to leave that with me," he said.

"How am I supposed to call my parents?"

"You'll have to work that out with your commanding officer." Hayden entered a series of commands into a control panel, and their hologram replicas disappeared. A moment later the flying spheres returned to their docking stations behind the counter.

Danielle looked at Colt like she wanted him to intervene, but he just shrugged. "It's just a phone," he said.

"My entire life is on that thing—all my pictures . . . contacts . . . a video of Wolfgang. How am I supposed to text anyone?"

⁙⁙⁙⁙⁙⁙⁙⁙⁙⁙⁙⁙⁙⁙⁙⁙⁙⁙⁙⁙⁙⁙

Colt looked over his shoulder as a very irritated Danielle disappeared behind a set of double doors that led to the women's locker room. For the first time since the night his parents died, he felt completely and utterly alone, and it was almost more than he could bear.

"This way, please," spoke the synthesized voice of a robot that stood patiently in the shadows—that is, if machines were capable of patience. It wasn't much taller than Colt, with glowing orange eyes set into a narrow head. Armored plates covered vital areas like its chest, shoulder joints, and pelvis, but the rest of the machine looked like a walking metal skeleton.

"I would like to take this opportunity to welcome you to the CHAOS Academy," it said as it shuffled down the dimly lit corridor. A light pulsed like a heartbeat from somewhere inside its chest, and Colt wondered if that was a critical part of its programming or something the designer added to give it the illusion of life. "I understand that you have experience with robotic life forms?"

"Yeah," Colt said, though he'd never heard that term before.

"Excellent." Its eyes actually lit brighter, and the voice sounded genuinely pleased. "I am an SVC-9 service bot, assembled at the Yoshikawa Corporation in March of this year. My artificial intelligence programming is unparalleled, and I am able to converse in over three hundred and twelve languages."

"I'm Colt, and I pretty much just speak one," he said. "I was taking Spanish, though."

The SVC-9 stopped at a door, and its eyes flickered in a rapid sequence—like some kind of combination—before it opened. "After you," it said, bowing slightly as Colt stepped through the threshold.

The room was about the size of Grandpa's garage, but instead of a lawn mower, spark plugs, or a rusted coffee can filled with mismatched nuts and bolts, there were hairbrushes and combs, shears, clippers, and three barber chairs that faced a giant mirror.

The door slid shut and Colt felt like an animal trapped in a cage.

"My sensors indicate that your heart rate is slightly elevated, and it would appear as though you have begun to perspire," SVC-9 said without inflection. "Is there a problem?"

"No," Colt said, but then he changed his mind. "Well, maybe."

"Please explain."

"It's just that . . . I mean . . ." He couldn't stop stammering. "Are you going to cut my hair or something?" It wasn't that Colt was vain. If anything, he really didn't care about his personal appearance. He was a good-looking kid, but his idea of fashion was anything that was comfortable—flip-flops, a worn T-shirt, board shorts or an old pair of jeans. But his hair? That was another story. He liked to wear it long, especially on top, but it looked like that was about to change.

"I'm afraid the current length of your hair does not fit within acceptable parameters," the machine said. "In order to be in compliance, it must not be excessive, ragged, unkempt, or extreme. Nor can it fall over your ears, your eyebrows, or touch the top of your shirt collar."

As Colt looked in the mirror, it was painfully obvious that his hair violated just about every one of those standards. He ran his fingers through his bangs and shook them out so they covered his forehead. They were definitely over his eyebrows. "Where should I sit?" he asked, resigned to his fate.

"Any chair will do," the machine said. "Do you know how you would like it styled? I've been trained in several techniques, and would be happy to—"

"Wait," Colt said. He was about to sit in the center chair. "*You're* going to cut my hair?" He looked down at the robot's hands, wondering how it would manage to hold the scissors. Besides, his last experience with a robot hadn't gone well. All it would take was a quick jab to the eye with the scissors, or maybe his ear or his neck, and game over.

"Does that surprise you?"

"Well, yeah, I guess," Colt said. "It's just that I didn't know robots actually cut hair."

"We can be programmed to serve any number of tasks, from simple assembly line duties to complex surgical procedures," the SVC-9 unit said. "Now if you don't mind, we're on a bit of a schedule. We still need to get you fitted into your uniform before the orientation begins."

Colt sat down, and the robot draped an apron around his neck so his hair wouldn't get on his clothes. Then, from some kind of relay system hidden behind its chest plate, it projected a hologram of Colt's disembodied head. The image cycled through a number of haircuts until Colt told it to stop. "That's it," he said. "I want that one."

"Very well."

Colt closed his eyes as the SVC-9 unit ran the clippers through his hair like a lawnmower cutting through grass that had been neglected for an entire summer. Thick shocks of wheat-colored locks fell to the floor.

"There you are." The robot held out a small mirror. "Would you like to see the back?"

"I doubt it looks any better than the front." Colt ran his hand over his scalp as the robot swept his discarded hair into a frighteningly large pile. Instant regret struck as he thought about what Lily would say, but then he remembered that it didn't matter. "I look ridiculous."

"You look like a soldier," the robot countered. "Now let's see about getting you some proper equipment to go with that haircut."

:: CHAPTER 29 ::

The SVC-9 unit escorted him into a locker room where a dozen or so boys milled around in various states of undress. Colt felt like he was walking into a wolves' den where the other males were trying to determine where he was going to fit in the pack.

A few of them were built like Olympic athletes, their bodies sculpted to near perfection, but not everyone looked like they had been synthetically designed in a laboratory. One boy couldn't have been taller than Colt's armpit, and Colt wasn't very tall to begin with. Another was so thin that he looked like a mad scientist had stretched a sheet of skin across a skeleton. He stood next to a kid who must have weighed close to three hundred pounds, and Colt wondered if he was going to have trouble making it through the physical training. Then again, he might have been brought in to be part of the information security team with Danielle.

"This way, please." The machine walked passed a bench where a wiry boy with blond hair was pulling a shirt over his head. It looked like it was made with neoprene, the material used to make wet suits.

"Is that what our uniform looks like?"

"Yes, but we'll get to that in a minute," the SVC-9 unit said as it stopped at what looked like a closet door. "Please disrobe."

"Here?"

"Your modesty is admirable, but I can assure you that there are no female specimens anywhere in the room." Without warning, the robot took him by the wrist, turned it over, and proceeded to stab the tip of his finger. It squeezed, drawing out a drop of blood that it collected before it released Colt's hand.

"Very good," the robot said as it pulled out a syringe and a vial that was filled with liquid so green it looked like sour apple hard candy.

"You're not thinking about sticking me with that, are you?"

"In fact, I am." The robot cleaned the meaty part of Colt's shoulder with a sterile pad before it jabbed him with the needle. It burned like acid, and it took all the self-control Colt could muster to keep from screaming.

"What is that?"

"A blend of vitamins and supplements that will help maximize your physical development."

"Like a steroid?"

"Not exactly. It's quite safe and rather legal, though I suppose the results will be similar." The machine discarded the needle in a medical waste bin and opened what looked like a closet door. It pulled out a white duffel bag with Colt's name and a black CHAOS insignia embroidered near the handles.

As Colt unzipped the bag, he saw the kid with blond hair talking to a tall cadet with a shaved head. He said something under his breath, and they both looked at Colt and laughed. Colt ignored them as he pulled out a shirt, pants, socks, underwear, boots, some kind of wristwatch, and what looked like aviator goggles.

"If you put it on, I will help you make the proper adjustments," the robot said.

Nothing fit quite right. The pant legs were too long, the waist was too big, and the sleeves hung past his wrists to the end of his fingertips. "Are you sure this is mine?" Colt asked.

"Quite."

The fabric started to shrink. "What's going on?" he asked, looking at his sleeves like they were covered in spiders.

"Your uniform is made using nanotechnology that allows us to control the fibers remotely," the machine said. "They are also equipped with sensors that relay your vital signs to our central computer, including your heart rate, body temperature, and other key data, such as your hydration level and your body fat composition, which is currently at two-point-four percent."

Colt ran his fingers over the surface of the fabric. It was smooth, like rubber, yet it felt soft and comfortable. He slid into the boots, which were a perfect fit, and turned to look at himself in the mirror.

The uniform was extremely white, with a thick black stripe that went from his sleeves up to his armpits and then down his side all the way to his boots. The only other design element was a CHAOS insignia on the chest. It looked like a cross between a superhero costume and something an astronaut might wear beneath his spacesuit. It was definitely a snug fit, but thanks to the padding his chest looked bigger and so did his shoulders.

He reached inside his bag and grabbed the wristwatch. It had a thick black band and an oversized face that looked like it was probably a video screen of some sort. Colt strapped it on and the screen flared to life, showing a CHAOS logo.

"As you may have guessed, that is your communicator," the SVC-9 unit said. "It will allow you to speak to your fellow cadets as well as any instructors. All messages are encrypted to protect our interests as an institution; however, you should know that your communications are monitored by staff as a safety precaution."

"What about these?" Colt asked, as he slipped the goggles over his head.

"Ah, yes," the machine said. "The goggles will not only protect your eyes against wind and particulates, but they are equipped with an advanced scanning technology."

"Scanning?"

The SVC-9 unit projected a hologram of a small creature with caramel-colored fur and enormous ears.

"Scanning object." The voice sounded like it had come from somewhere inside the goggles, and Colt watched as a complicated wire frame formed around the creature. The splines were green, and there was a series of words that flashed as though the goggles were cycling through some kind of database, looking for the right entry. "This specimen is known as a Moklok. Native to the forests on the planet Nemus, they are reclusive and territorial. However, they are not considered dangerous unless provoked."

"How do the goggles know what to scan?"

"Over time they will grow accustomed to your thought patterns, but for now all you need to do is focus on an object and the goggles will do the rest."

"What's next?"

"Orientation."

He started to follow the robot toward the door, but the kid

with the blond hair asked him to hold up. According to the patch on his shirt, his name was Bowen. He was an inch or two taller than Colt, with a sharp nose and green eyes flecked with gold.

"Hey, were you in the van that ran that guy off the road?"

Colt looked at him, wondering how he'd found out.

Bowen smiled with a confidence that bordered on cocky. "Our driver got a call after he picked us up at the airport," he said, as though it should have been obvious. "He told us that it was one of the shapeshifters. Is that true?"

"We didn't stick around to find out," Colt said, uncomfortable with the direction their conversation was heading. He didn't know what it was, but something about Bowen rubbed him the wrong way.

"Come along," the SVC-9 called over its shoulder. "We don't want to be late."

:: CHAPTER 30 ::

The amphitheatre was perfectly round with rows of tiered seating that looked down on a stage far below. There were at least five hundred chairs, most of which were empty, but cadets continued to stream through the doors that lined the outer wall. Most stuck to the shadows toward the back, but a few ventured up front. Colt figured they were the overachievers, eager to make a good first impression.

The room was basically divided in half, girls on one side and boys on the other, like a junior high dance. He smiled, wondering how long it would take everyone to forget about girlfriends and boyfriends back home, but that made him think about Lily, and once again he felt sick about the way he had left things. There was nothing he could do about it now.

He was about to sit down when Danielle walked in with Ms. Skoglund. Her uniform looked like his, white with the black stripe down the side. Her hair was pulled back into a ponytail and her goggles were perched on top of her forehead. The two of them hugged, and Danielle walked down the steps to sit next to a group of girls while Ms. Skoglund sat in what looked like the teacher section. Giru Ba was there as well, but she was on the far end of the row.

"No wonder I couldn't find you."

Colt turned around and saw Oz loping down the stairs. Somehow the uniform made him look even bigger, if that was possible. It fit snugly around the contours of his muscles, looking more like skin than clothing. He took his enormous hands and placed them on top of Colt's head, rubbing it like it was a magic lamp.

"Knock it off," Colt said, pushing him away.

"I can't believe you went cue ball." Oz took the seat next to Colt. "You know you didn't have to do that, right?"

"It's just hair. It'll grow back."

Oz shrugged. "Anyway, it looks like your little incident on the parkway made the news. Some guy took a video of the accident and posted it online. The driver of that car you ran off the road had green blood pouring out of his forehead. You know what that means, right?"

"Yeah, he's a shapeshifter."

"You don't seem surprised."

Colt shrugged. "Danielle ran the number on the license plate," Colt said, watching Oz to see how he would react. "It was registered to Aldrich Koenig, but we don't think he was the one driving."

"Maybe one of his guys went rogue and decided to come after you."

"Maybe."

There were footsteps, and Colt turned to see a cadet with green skin standing in the doorway. His hair was—well, it was actually tentacles, and they were swept back over his head like dreadlocks. He wore enormous goggles along with some kind of breathing apparatus filled with bubbling water. It was connected to a pair of tanks that hung on his back like scuba gear, and even though they looked heavy, he didn't seem to mind.

"Name's Bar-Ryak. He's Undarian," Oz said. "They live under-water, so he needs the tanks to breathe whenever he's on land."

"He's one of the cadets?" Colt asked. "But he's . . . you know."

"An alien?" Oz smiled. "What was your first clue?"

The house lights dimmed, and a thin man wearing a black military uniform walked to the center of the stage, his heels click-ing on the tile with every step. The room turned deathly quiet as he stood with his hands behind his back. His hair was cut short and neatly combed to the side, his cheekbones were gaunt, and his face lacked even the slightest hit of warmth.

"Welcome to the CHAOS Military Academy," he said with impeccable diction. "My name is Agent Reginald Graves, and it is my honor to welcome you to this prestigious institution." He paused, his eyes roving the room as he walked in a slow circle. "For decades, our agents have worked in the shadows, protecting mankind from supernatural forces that were once thought to be nothing more than myth and legend. But as recent events have proven, the likes of aliens, wolf men, and others of their ilk are all but too real.

"World leaders have assured the masses that we have every-thing under control. They have repeated time and again that the gateways opened by the Thule on September 24 of this year have not only been sealed shut, but that we have locked the doors and thrown away the proverbial keys."

Agent Graves folded his hands and placed his long index fingers against his lips. "I am afraid that those gateways are the least of our concerns. You see, we believe the Thule are nearing completion on a machine that will allow them to create traversable wormholes—a kind of bridge that connects two points in the universe. Once that happens, they will fill our skies with warships and hunt us until we are extinct."

The cadets fidgeted uncomfortably.

"Ladies and gentlemen, you have been summoned in the middle of our term because time is running short. Not only are you the youngest class in the history of this institution, but there is also a chance that you will be among the last class who passes through these halls. Our hope . . . indeed, our prayer is that you will rise up and lead us to victory. If not, we may be in the last days of our existence as a species."

Oz stood and clapped. At first, the other cadets looked confused, but then someone a few seats away stood with him. So did another, and then another. Before long, everyone was standing and cheering. Agent Graves stood there, his face stoic as he allowed the applause to crescendo. Then, like a conductor before an orchestra, he raised his hands and everyone stopped.

"Very good," he said. "Given the special circumstances that have brought us together, Director Romero has asked if he could say a few words. Director?"

There was a flicker like a lightbulb, and suddenly Oz's dad was standing in the middle of the stage—only he wasn't actually there. It was a hologram. "I'm sorry I couldn't be there to greet you in person," he said. "But as you can imagine, my schedule has been a bit hectic lately.

"I won't repeat what you've heard from Agent Graves, but it's critical that you understand what's at stake. The Thule are warmongers. They have stripped their world of its natural resources and now they have to find a new home or they'll face extinction. We believe that they picked Earth because our atmosphere is similar to theirs, but we're not going to let that happen."

Lobo paused and took a deep breath. "I'll shoot straight with you. Thanks to a generation of politicians more interested in self-preservation than the good of mankind, our program has been woefully underfunded for decades. That means our military, as well as this agency, is not equipped with the tools, much less the bodies needed to protect our planet against the inevitable. But giving up isn't an option!

"That means we're going to push you to your breaking point, and then we're going to push you harder. And when you feel like quitting, I want you to remember that you are humanity's last line of defense. We won't have time to train another class of cadets before the Thule arrive, so if you fail, we'll be wiped from the history books. Sleep well tonight, because starting tomorrow, life as you know it will change forever."

There was applause, and Lobo's figure flickered and disappeared as Agent Graves returned to the stage to review academy rules. Most were fairly obvious, like boys weren't allowed in the girls' dorms and vice versa. Nobody could leave school grounds without prior authorization, and cadets were expected to be in class on time. No exceptions.

"There will be no personal electronic devices—that goes for phones, music players, laptops, and cameras—all are strictly forbidden." The cadets started to complain, but Agent Graves simply raised his hand and waited for everyone to calm down. "There is too much at stake to risk leaking critical data to the public at large. However, each of you will be given a tablet computer loaded with your textbooks."

Someone in the back of the room raised his hand and cleared his throat. He was sitting with a cluster of boys, most of whom were trying to hide the fact that they were laughing.

"Name, please," Agent Graves said, his cold eyes regarding the cadet.

"It's Pierce, but most people call me—"

"I did not ask for a nickname," Agent Graves said, cutting him off. His manner was calm, but he spoke with an unquestioned authority. "And when you speak, you will stand and speak with conviction. Now try again."

"Pierce Bowen."

Colt rolled his eyes. It was the annoying kid from the locker room.

"Ah, yes," Agent Graves said with a nod. "Your father is the junior senator from Utah. He was a rising star until reports surfaced that he was having an affair."

Pierce clenched his jaw, but he didn't say anything.

"Trust is a critical part of this organization." Agent Graves paused for a moment. "Are you trustworthy, or do you believe that your genetics will betray you?"

Pierce seethed, his face bright red as his eyes shifted to the other cadets who were sitting around him. They slouched in their seats before Agent Graves decided to bring up their family secrets as well.

"I'm sorry, I don't believe I heard your response," Agent Graves said.

"Yes, sir. You can trust me."

"I certainly hope so," the agent said. "Now I believe you had a question."

Colt wondered if the instructors tore the cadets down before they built them back up as part of the training. Why else would he publicly humiliate Pierce like that? Or maybe Agent Graves was just a jerk. He'd find out soon enough.

"I wanted to know if everyone here has had their blood tested," Pierce said.

"Tested?" Agent Graves said. "What do you mean?"

Pierce looked around the room to make sure he had a captive audience. "My father is a member of the Senate Committee on Intelligence, and he told me what really happened in Iowa. There wasn't a leak in that nuclear reactor—someone released a virus, and that's why they quarantined the city—they didn't want it to spread."

"An interesting theory," Agent Graves said.

"It's not a theory. I've seen pictures of people who were infected, and they all died within forty-eight hours," Pierce said. "The virus wasn't contained. They found it in Thailand and Mexico, and there's been another outbreak in Haiti. And the scary part? There's no cure, because it didn't come from our world. It's a biological weapon from the Thule, so before they try to sneak into this facility and spread the virus through the air ducts or something, I figured we should know if anyone here is a shape-shifter in disguise."

Colt gripped his chair until his knuckles turned white. Did Pierce know his secret?

olt fought an overwhelming urge to jump out of his chair and rush to the nearest mirror. He wanted to make sure his skin hadn't started to morph into scales and that his eyes were still blue instead of that creepy yellow color.

"What's wrong with you?" Oz asked as everyone left the amphitheatre.

"Nothing."

"Then why do you look like you're about to throw up?"

"Do you think he's right?"

"That one of us is a shapeshifter?" Oz asked. "I doubt it. They wouldn't get passed the security scan in the lobby—their skeletal structure is different, even after they shape-shift into a human form. Besides, everyone has to get a blood test."

Colt followed Oz toward a group of about twenty cadets, each looking unsure. When he saw their tour guide, he understood why. The giant was at least seven feet tall and covered in fur that was the color of rust. Intense eyes hid beneath a heavy brow, its nose was short—almost like a dog's—and it had a wide jaw that looked strong enough to crush boulders.

All of that would have been enough to terrify anyone, but the creature looked like a mad scientist had twisted it into some kind of a hybrid. Its left arm had been replaced by a robotic prosthetic, with working fingers and joints. Its right leg was mechanical as well, but the strangest enhancement was a second head that sat just above its prosthetic arm. It was cased in metal and had a glowing eye that roved back and forth, scanning the cadets.

"Remember him?" Oz asked.

Colt nodded. The last time they had seen Lohr, they were at Hyde Field House as a guest of Basil Hyde, a former CHAOS agent turned businessman. Amongst his many enterprises, Hyde owned and operated the Intergalactic Fighting League. It was similar to boxing or mixed martial arts, but the IGFL pitted the greatest fighters in the twelve known worlds against one another—and Lohr was ranked toward the top of his weight class. He was also the combat training instructor at the CHAOS Military Academy.

"Now that we're all here, let's go over some rules," Lohr said, his voice deep and rich. "Anyone in a black uniform is an instructor, and you'll address them as sir or ma'am. If you see someone in a gray uniform, that's a second-year cadet. They've been here longer than you, and they've earned certain privileges. When you see one walking down the path, you step aside and let them pass. Other than that, I have only have one rule . . . do exactly what I say when I say it, and you won't have to sleep in the infirmary tonight."

Lohr led them through the halls of the main building, which felt more like a warehouse or an industrial park. He explained that it was a façade, and how delivery drivers and postal workers thought that the CHAOS Military Academy was actually the Morrow Research Institute, a facility that specialized in the study of infectious diseases. It was the perfect cover, because nobody stuck around long enough to see more than the lobby or the loading dock. They were too worried about catching anthrax, SARS, or Legionnaires' disease to notice the rest of the campus.

The grounds housed what used to be a private university founded by Thomas Jefferson in the 1820s that was patterned after the College of William and Mary, which he attended as a young man. The school specialized in history, mathematics, metaphysics, and philosophy, as well as foreign languages and music. It boasted an enormous library, housing Jefferson's vast collection of books, but the school found hard times during the Great Depression and shuttered the doors in 1937. It wasn't long after that the United States Army purchased the land, where it was turned into a training ground for their top secret CHAOS program.

It was closing in on seven o'clock, and the sun was already gone as they left the warmth of the building for a network of lighted paths. Colt could see the steam rising from his lips, and he started to wonder if the cadets would be given some kind of jacket, or at least a windbreaker. Then it started to feel like his uniform was actually heating up.

"The fibers are programmed to elevate your body temperature when it drops below normal," Oz said when he saw the strange look on Colt's face.

They cut through a series of buildings made of stone and brick, all with steep steps and tall pillars. Some were dedicated to traditional subjects, but there were also buildings for espionage, combat, and weapons systems. Eventually they came to a recreational center that had gymnasiums, racquetball courts, and weight rooms. There was a massive library, a chapel with a cemetery out back, a theatre, and combat simulation rooms where cadets trained with holograms.

They had rounded the corner of a grassy area covered with trees to discover a stadium lit up with hundreds of lights. Cadets cut through the sky in jet packs, flying through metal rings that somehow hovered in the air. One did a back flip while two others looked like they were racing around a series of floating pylons. But there were more than jet packs. Other cadets went around on some kind of a surfboard, only instead of sliding across the water they soared three feet off the ground.

"Welcome to the flight center," Lohr said.

"What are those?" Colt asked.

"Hoverboards," Oz said. "They can't fly as high or as fast as a jet pack, but they're a lot better for distance."

"How do they work?"

"I don't know," Oz said with a shrug. "It has something to do with the earth's gravitational pull. I think the technical term is electrostatic repulsion. There's an electric charge on the bottom of the board, and it repels the charge on the earth's surface."

"Looks like fun."

The group started heading back to the main building, but Colt lingered, watching hoverboard riders veer through an obstacle course. He hadn't been surfing since the day his parents died, and that was almost three months ago.

"Come on, McAlister," he heard Oz call. "I'm hungry, and I'm going to blame you if all the good food is gone before we get to the party."

:: CHAPTER 32 ::

C olt followed the group back inside. The warm air brushed his cheek as the sliding door closed behind him, but despite the cold he wanted to go back and watch the hoverboards. Maybe he would sneak away unnoticed once everyone was busy eating. Then again, the doors were probably going to be monitored.

Lohr led them through a network of corridors, his head just inches from the ceiling tiles as they passed door after door, each requiring a biometric scan to access whatever was inside. One of the cadets placed his hand on a pad to see what would happen. Red lights formed around his fingertips and a sensor beeped twice, but that was it.

They passed through a set of double doors and into a passage that looked like an acrylic tube. It cut through an enormous aquarium, just like the shark encounter at Sea World. Exotic marine life swam overhead on either side as the cadets watched in wonder. There was a school of fish that looked a bit like barracuda. They were long and thin, with erratic teeth that poked out from their jaws like quills on a porcupine. Their scales were bright red, like the skin of an apple, with yellow striping that cut horizontally across their snakelike bodies.

The tube opened into a viewing theatre that was as big as two gymnasiums sitting side by side. There was a wall of glass that was at least a hundred feet wide by thirty feet high, and inside a forest of kelp swayed back and forth in the current as strange creatures swam in and out of view.

"Welcome to the Jules Verne Aquatic Center," Lohr said, as waitstaff in crisp white tuxedo jackets crisscrossed the floor carrying trays laden with food. "Tonight you'll dine as our guests, but don't get used to the service or the food. As Director Romero said, we're going to push you to your breaking point and beyond. So enjoy it while you can." He paused, looking each cadet in the eye to drive the point home. "Some of you are going to flame out, but others will thrive. And when we're done with you, you *will* lead us to victory over the shapeshifters. Now go and eat."

Strange music cascaded through the speakers as the cadets made their way inside. It was both beautiful and haunting, as though it had been composed in another world. The center of the floor was set with rows of round tables covered in white linen, and there were buffets laden with food along the outer walls. As they walked passed, Colt saw rice pilaf with slivered almonds, asparagus spears, and a carving station with prime rib, au jus, and creamy horseradish sauce. But there were also foods he had never seen before—sautéed mushroom caps that were bright orange with yellow spots, wriggling creatures that looked like tiny squid, and fruits with spiny husks and juicy flesh.

Oz grabbed two plates, balancing the second on the back of

his forearm as he took at least a little of everything. Colt wasn't feeling as adventurous, though he decided after some coaxing to put one of the squid on his plate. It flipped and twisted like it was trying to escape, and Colt's stomach churned when he saw it looking back at him with desperate eyes.

"Have you seen Danielle?" Oz asked as he plucked two of the squid off his plate and plopped them in his mouth.

Colt scanned the room and saw her sitting at a table near the enormous glass wall, sitting next to a girl with ginger hair cropped to her shoulders. "Yeah, she's over there."

The boys wound through the room, passing a table where instructors ate hors d'oeuvres and sipped a dark liquid that looked like a cross between grape juice and maple syrup.

"Hello, ladies," Oz said as he flashed a smile. "Mind if we join you?" He didn't wait for a response as he took the seat next to Danielle.

Her eyes lit up when she saw Colt's head. At first she looked confused, but then she started laughing. She covered her mouth and turned away, trying to stop, but she couldn't help it.

"Go ahead, get it out of your system," Colt said. His hand went to the top of his head and he started rubbing the stubble.

"I'm sorry," she said, trying to regain her composure. "It's just that . . . I mean . . ." She fumbled over her words and laughed until her eyes were filled with tears. "I'm just not used to seeing you without hair, that's all," she finally managed to say. "But I think you look . . . well, you look great."

"No, I don't," Colt said. "I look like a freak."

"What happened?" asked the girl with the ginger hair, and Colt blushed.

"Pretty boy here used to have long hair," Oz said. "You

know, like a surfer. But he decided to go cue ball, and now he's regretting his decision."

"It's just hair," Danielle said, the smile leaving her lips.

"Whatever," Colt said, ready to turn the spotlight on someone else. If it were up to him, he would have headed to his dorm room, but they hadn't been assigned yet.

"Anyway, this is Stacy," Danielle said. "And these are the guys I was telling you about."

The girl waved, but her eyes lingered on Colt for a moment before she turned away. It made him feel uncomfortable, though he wasn't sure why. She was beautiful, and it wasn't like he had a girlfriend. So why did it feel like he was cheating on Lily, just because some girl he didn't know smiled at him?

"So you were talking about us?" Oz asked as he leaned forward.

Danielle rolled her eyes as Oz cut into his prime rib, dipped it into a pool of creamy horseradish sauce, and took a bite.

"What's your story?" he asked as he looked at Stacy, ignoring the rule where you aren't supposed to talk with food in your mouth. "You know, where are you from and that stuff?"

"You must be Oz," Stacy said.

"Guilty."

"I tell you what. Why don't you tell me *your* story, and if it's interesting, I'll tell you mine."

Oz stopped with the fork in his mouth and smiled. "All right," he said. "My name is Oswaldo Alexander Romero, I was born right here in Virginia, and I like romantic comedies, books about sparkling vampires, and long walks on the beach."

"Cute," she said. "Of course, even if I believed you, you'd have to dig a little deeper if you want me to talk."

Oz shrugged. "My dad's the director of CHAOS, so I've seen

a lot of crazy stuff. I've been to three planets, I like video games where you get to blow stuff up, and the only way I'll read a book is if it has lots of pictures."

"What, like comic books?"

"I'm in my local shop every Wednesday."

Stacy's eyes lit up. "Really? What do you read?"

"I don't know," he said. "The usual, I guess. Stuff like the *Fantastic Four. X-Men. Justice League.*"

"What about the *Phantom Flyer*?"

Oz looked at her sideways and pointed at Colt with his fork. "You know who his grandpa is, right?"

"Should I?"

"Um, yeah. He's the Phantom Flyer—as in the real deal."

Stacy frowned as though she might have misunderstood, but then a smile broke out. "You're the kid who brought down Trident?"

Colt looked away, embarrassed, as his neck flushed bright red.

"Don't be shy," Oz said as he wrapped his massive arm around Colt's neck, pulling him close. "You're famous."

"Knock it off," Colt said, pushing him away.

There was a loud crash as plates shattered near one of the buffets. Everyone turned to see the green-skinned Undarian sitting on the floor, his uniform smeared with sauce as Pierce Bowen stood over him, laughing.

"Nice move, freak show!" Pierce said.

Colt pushed through the crowd until he was standing between Pierce and the alien. "Are you okay?" he asked, offering Bar-Ryak his hand.

"I'm fine, thank you."

Pierce grabbed Colt by the arm and swung him around. "What are you doing? That thing knocked in to *me*!"

"I'm sure it was an accident." Colt grabbed Pierce by the wrist, applying pressure with his thumb until he let go.

"The only reason you'd care is if you were one of them," Pierce said, his eyes boiling.

⁙⁙⁙⁙⁙⁙⁙⁙⁙⁙⁙⁙⁙⁙⁙⁙⁙⁙⁙⁙⁙⁙⁙

"You realize that you just made an enemy, right?" Oz said as they walked back to the table. He sat down, grabbed a dinner roll, and used it to sop up a pool of gravy.

Colt shrugged as Oz plopped the roll into his mouth and licked his fingers.

"Don't get me wrong, I admire what you did," Oz said. "I'm just saying that you better sleep with one eye open. That's all."

"Trust me, I already do."

"Which is why you and I are going to be roommates."

"Seriously?"

"Have I ever lied to you?"

Colt hesitated, not wanting to answer the question. He didn't know what to think anymore. There was a good chance that Oz had been lying to him since the day they met, but he had no way to prove it—at least not yet. Then again, Oz was acting like everything was normal between them.

Oz frowned when Colt didn't answer, but the moment passed. He shrugged, looked at the empty dinner plates in front of him, and stood up. "I don't know about you guys, but I'm ready for seconds," he said. He headed back to the buffet line.

"I'll join you," Stacy said. "I think I saw some chocolate cake. Do you want to come?"

"In a minute." Danielle slid into the chair next to Colt and lowered her voice. "Let me see your communicator."

"Why?"

She looked over her shoulder. "We don't have a lot of time."

Colt wasn't sure what she was up to, but he unfastened the strap and handed it to her. "So are you going to tell me what you're doing, or do I have to guess?"

"Is anybody coming?" she asked as her fingers tapped feverishly on the buttons.

Colt tried to be discreet as he glanced around. Oz was at the carving station with Stacy, who was holding an enormous slice of chocolate cake. Pierce was over in the corner, probably plotting his revenge, and everyone else was distracted by their own conversations. Then he spotted Agent Graves. He was looking their way and frowning as though he knew Danielle was up to something, but she had her back turned to him, so it would have been difficult for him to see what she was doing.

"How much longer?" Colt asked.

"I'm almost done." When Danielle was finished, she wrapped the communicator in a napkin and handed it back to him. "CHAOS monitors everything that goes through these things, but Ms. Skoglund gave me a code that will encrypt our transmissions so we can have some privacy whenever we need it. Just make sure you activate it before you send me something that you don't want anyone else to see."

Colt unwrapped the communicator and put it back on his wrist. "Do you trust her?"

"Who, Ms. Skoglund?"

"It's just kind of weird. I mean, she showed up with those files out of nowhere, and ever since then things have gotten kind of crazy."

"Things were already crazy," Danielle said. "Besides, your grandpa trusts her, right? Otherwise he wouldn't have told her where to find you the other night."

"I guess," Colt said, more confused than ever. He decided to join Oz and get some more of the prime rib, but as he stood up he realized that Agent Graves was still staring their way.

:: CHAPTER 33 ::

The boys' dormitory was a three-story brick building that stood across from the library, separated from it by a small pond. Smoke wafted from a pair of chimneys, offering the promise of warmth as the snow continued to fall across campus. The walkway was lined with a trail of footprints as the cadets marched silently, heads down, as they were ushered up the steps and inside.

The front door opened to a large room that looked like some kind of parlor. A fire crackled inside a hearth that was flanked by a sofa and a few chairs. The rest of the room was filled with tables that sat six, and Colt figured it was a study room. Portraits of former academy instructors hung on the wall, most of them old men with piercing eyes and a cluster of medals hanging on their jackets.

"Let's go!" the instructor shouted as the cadets filed in. His name was Agent Nixon, and he couldn't have been much older than twenty-five, with dark eyes and darker hair that he kept short and combed to the side. Unlike the cadets, he was wearing a black uniform, though it had the same CHAOS insignia over the left breast pocket. "You all have your room assignments. Everything you'll need is waiting in your dresser drawer—for some, there might even be a pacifier to keep you from crying all night."

The cadets laughed as they trudged up the steps, leaving a trail of mud and snow that didn't go unnoticed. "Now I don't know about you, but I was taught to wipe my shoes on the mat before I walked inside someone's home," Agent Nixon said. He grabbed the closest cadet by the collar, a lanky kid named Grey Allen who refused to look him in the eye. "Did you wipe your feet, Cadet Allen?"

"Yes, sir," the kid said, his voice hardly a whisper as he tried to keep from falling down.

"Then where did that trail of mud come from?"

Grey was so frightened that his mouth was moving, but no words came out. All he could do was make a series of strange sounds as Agent Nixon rolled his eyes and sent him to get a bucket and mop.

One of the house rules was that first-year cadets weren't allowed to use the elevators, so Oz led Colt up two flights of stairs and stopped at a door at the end of the hall. He placed his enormous hand on a biometric sensor, and his fingertips lit green as the door clicked open. "Welcome home."

It was smaller than Colt's bedroom back in Arizona, but somehow they'd managed to pack in two bunk beds and a single dresser with four narrow drawers.

"You're kidding, right?" Colt said. "There're going to be four of us in here?"

"Relax." Oz walked over and pressed his thumb against a small sensor on the top drawer, and it lit orange. "We're just here to sleep," he said. "If you aren't training or eating, you'll spend most of your time down in the study lounge." He placed his thumb against the sensor again, and this time it lit green. The drawer opened, and inside were a second uniform, enough socks and underwear to last a week, some toiletries like deodorant, a toothbrush, some toothpaste, and a small silver case that wasn't much larger than a hardback novel.

Oz pulled it out and sat down on one of the bottom bunks with his back against the wall and his long legs hanging over the side. He removed the metal case, and underneath was a sleek tablet computer with a touch screen. "Most of the campus is a dead zone, so you can't go on the Internet, but Danielle said she'd help us try to find a way around."

The door opened and two more cadets walked in. The first was Grey, the kid who got stuck mopping up after everyone. He took the top bunk, leaving the bottom for Ethan Foley, who had recently moved back to the States after spending a few years in Dubai, where his father had overseen the construction of a luxury resort that boasted the world's largest swimming pool.

Colt looked at the clock on the dresser. He didn't feel much like conversation, and there were still twenty minutes before lights out, so he decided to get some fresh air. "I'll be back in a while," he said.

"Where are you going?"

"I don't know. I just want to clear my head."

Snow covered the landscape in a blanket of white as he walked down the winding path that led past the girls' dormitory. He wondered how Danielle was getting along with the other girls, and if she had already found a way to patch into the school's network so she could send an e-mail to her parents. She'd never been gone from home for more than a week, and that was to a summer camp with the youth group at her church. Since her mom was one of the chaperones, Colt figured that didn't count.

Right now everything seemed like an adventure, but in a few days the reality of the commitment that it took to be a cadet was bound to sink in. The walls around the school grounds were meant to do more than keep unwanted guests from getting inside; they also made sure that nobody wandered away.

Colt crossed under the shadow of a bell tower that rose above the chapel. In a few minutes the bell would ring ten times, and at that point the cadets were expected to be in their rooms, lights off and quiet. He thought about heading back; after all, he didn't want to get in trouble on his first day. But just then he heard the sound of feet shuffling down the path toward him.

He skirted off the path and slipped into a cluster of trees where he could see the headstones in the cemetery. The canopy of branches kept most of the snow at bay, but the ground was covered in rotting leaves that crunched with each step, making any attempt at stealth nearly impossible.

It wasn't long before he saw two figures walking down the path, shoulders hunched and heads down. Colt felt the hair on the back of his neck stand on end, and his heart started to pound inside his chest. That only happened when Krone was around, but the person on the left was Agent Graves, and he was walking with Giru Ba, who didn't look anything like one of the Thule. So where was Krone?

Colt tried to shift his weight, but as he did his heel came down on a dead branch.

Agent Graves stopped. "Did you hear that?"

"It was probably just the wind," Giru Ba said.

"I don't think so. It came from over there." He pointed directly to where Colt was hiding.

"I don't see anything," she said.

Agent Graves took a step toward the trees, and for a moment Colt thought he'd been spotted. He held his breath and considered running, but Agent Graves turned and headed down the path with Giru Ba, back toward the main building.

Colt exhaled, but he didn't relax—not if Krone was out there somewhere watching him. Besides, according to the clock on his wrist communicator, there were only a few minutes until lights out. His only chance was to cut through the woods and hope he didn't get turned around.

He forged deeper into the cluster of trees, hoping that he could reach the dorm before he ran into Krone. The moon was little more than a sliver in the night sky, offering precious little light as he tried to avoid gnarled roots and annoying bushes with nasty thorns.

Something moved in the distance, and he spun to see the silhouette of a raccoon scamper into a tree. Relieved, he shook his head and exhaled, wondering why he had gone on the walk in the first place. It felt like the temperature had dropped at least ten degrees, and even though the heated fibers of his uniform kept him relatively warm, he was ready to crawl into bed and fall asleep beneath his wool blanket.

He kept walking, keeping the rushing water from the Potomac River off to the right, but he should have found the dorm by now. There wasn't enough time to backtrack and make it to his room before curfew, so he decided to make for a nearby hill, hoping that would give him a clear view of the campus.

Distracted, he didn't notice rotting slats of wood that spanned what looked like some kind of mine shaft. The boards creaked at the weight of his step before they snapped. Colt had no idea what had happened as he fell into the darkness.

The impact sent the air rushing from his lungs, and he groaned, disoriented as he writhed on the ground. He rolled over and forced himself to sit up. Remnants of moonlight slipped through a narrow opening that was at least ten feet up.

The minute remaining before curfew was the least of his problems. From what he could see, he had fallen into a tunnel. The walls were curved, and so was the ceiling, so climbing back out would be difficult, if not impossible. He tapped on the display of his wrist communicator, trying to reach Danielle, but he couldn't get it to work underground. Frustrated, he wondered who had built the tunnel, and why. Thoughts of subterranean monsters filled his head, but he pushed them away as he tried to determine which direction to take. There was no point of reference, which meant one direction was as good as the next. He decided to go left.

Unable to see, he used the wall as his guide. It was damp and cold, and he could feel the hairy roots of the trees sticking out from the dirt surface. Panic tried to grab hold of him with each step, but Colt pushed forward, knowing that his only other option was to sit where he'd fallen through and wait for morning. Even then, there was no guarantee that anyone would find him.

He was about to give up when his hand fell on what felt like a ladder that was bolted to the wall. When he got to the top, he found another wooden grate. With one arm locked around the rungs, he pressed his hand against the slats. They resisted at first, but with a little effort he was able to push them away. He was in a well—or at least something that was built to look like a well. The library was nearby, which meant he was close to the dorm. There was only one problem. He was past curfew.

His first thought was to try and get hold of Oz using his

communicator, but he forgot how to scramble the message, and if their transmissions were monitored, the staff would know he had broken the rules. He decided to at least try the doors to see if they were unlocked.

He crawled out of the well and headed back toward the dorm, but stopped when he saw someone standing on the front step. "I was starting to think that you wouldn't make it," Giru Ba said.

Colt glanced about the shadows, looking for Agent Graves.

"Don't worry," she said. "I'm alone."

"What are you doing here?" he asked.

"That answer is more complicated than you might think. For now, let's just say I thought you might need a bit of help."

:: CHAPTER 34 ::

C olt woke up the next morning with his bed shaking violently. Not knowing if it was an attack or an earthquake, he jumped out of the top bunk and onto the floor. His eyes were wild as he stood in a crouch, his tired brain trying to assess whether he should run or stay and fight.

It didn't register that someone was laughing until he saw Oz. "What are you doing?" he asked as he stood in his boxer briefs.

"Consider it your wake-up call." Oz walked over and flipped on the lights. "Hurry up and get dressed or you're going to miss breakfast."

"What time is it?" Colt asked as he looked outside the window. It was dark, and the moon was still out, though it was hidden behind a bank of gray clouds.

"Almost five thirty."

Breakfast wasn't anything like the feast they had eaten the night before, but it was better than Colt expected. There were scrambled eggs—the real kind, not that powdered mix like they served at summer camp—along with sausage, oatmeal, and whole grain toast. They even provided energy drinks.

"You better take two." Oz grabbed a second from the cooler and placed it on Colt's tray. "What's with you, anyway? Were you up all night or something?"

Colt shrugged. "Kind of. I'm not used to the mattress." He wasn't about to mention how he had seen Agent Graves and Giru Ba, that he was almost certain Krone had been tracking him on campus, or how he'd fallen into some kind of tunnel. None of it made sense.

He needed to talk to Danielle, but she wasn't in the dining hall. Most of the cadets had already left for their first-hour classes. He spotted Pierce in the back of the room, hunched over as he whispered something to the other cadets at his table. Colt made eye contact for a moment, then turned away, picking a chair so that Pierce was stuck looking at his back.

He ate quickly, wondering how he was going to keep from falling asleep in class. He barely had the energy to keep his eyes open, much less walk from one building to the next. "I'd do anything for a mocha cappuccino with an extra shot of espresso," he said as one of the service bots took his empty plate.

Oz grabbed an energy drink, cracked the lid, and plopped it down in front of Colt. "I'm telling you, one of these will wake you up. Two will make you think that you can fly."

Colt brought it to his nose and sniffed. "It smells like an orange Creamsicle." He took a swig, and the effects were almost immediate. It was like someone had injected caffeine straight into his bloodstream. His fingers and toes started to tingle, and his eyes opened wide. "What's in this thing?" he asked, looking at the label.

"I don't know. But whatever it is, it works."

According to the schedule, their first class was Basic Combat

Techniques. The building was on the other side of campus, on a hill that overlooked the Potomac River. It looked like one of those warehouse clubs, except instead of metal shelves crammed with bulk food items, everything inside was dedicated to the art of self-defense. Lohr stood in one of the boxing rings with a cluster of cadets, including Danielle and Stacy, waiting for class to begin. Colt wanted to pull Danielle aside to tell her what had happened, but he didn't get a chance before the bell rang.

"All right, listen up," Lohr said, his deep voice cutting through the chatter. "I'm supposed to teach you how to defend yourselves against monsters that make me look like a furry little kitten, but most of you wouldn't even last thirty seconds with your own grandmothers."

A few of the cadets laughed.

"Somehow, some way, I'm going to mold each one of you into a living weapon capable of things that you never dreamed possible—but you're going to have to do your part. That means total dedication from the moment you walk into this gym until the time you leave. If the Thule are on their way, as we think they are, then there's a good chance you'll be the last batch of recruits that will have time to train. So if you fail, we all die."

Nobody made a sound.

"Today we're going to pair up and do a little sparring," he said. "I've seen your files, but as far as I'm concerned a black belt doesn't mean anything, and I couldn't care less if you were on the varsity wrestling team back home. I want to see what you can do with my own two eyes, so let's have Romero and Jomtong front and center."

"Nice," Oz said. "His dad was a Muay Thai champion. This should be fun." He had a wide grin as he climbed into the ring.

Colt wasn't sure that fighting Jomtong would be his idea of fun. He watched him walk up the steps and slide between the ropes. The cadet was thin but muscular, and even though he was eight inches shorter and nearly a hundred pounds lighter than Oz, he didn't look nervous. In fact, his eyes smoldered like a mongoose eyeing a king cobra.

"Before any of you start complaining about the size differential, you need to understand something," Lohr said. "There's no such thing as a fair fight, so you might as well accept it and move on. There will always be someone bigger and stronger, which means you need to use your head, not just your fists, knees, and elbows." He looked at Oz, then Jomtong, and he smiled. "Are you two ready?"

They both nodded.

"Fight!"

They circled around the center of the ring, looking for an opening. Oz feigned with his right hand, pulled back, and struck. The quick jab would have knocked Jomtong across the ring, but Jomtong was too quick. He connected with a straight foot thrust to Oz's stomach, knocking him off balance. Then he ran and jumped, using Oz's thigh as a springboard. His knee bashed into Oz's jaw, and with a loud crack, Oz fell to the mat.

"See what I mean?" Lohr stepped between them. He offered his hand, but Oz pushed it away and walked to the center of the ring. "You're sure you want to go through that again?"

Oz nodded as Jomtong stood in front of him, fists held high.

"It's your funeral," Lohr said. "Fight!"

This time Oz waited for Jomtong to make the first move. The smaller boy kicked, but Oz caught his ankle with his arm and drove his elbow into Jomtong's thigh. Jomtong pulled away, limping, but he didn't back down. Instead, he did a handstand and hit Oz in the chest with his knee. Then he bounced back to his feet, threw a spinning elbow, and followed it with an ax heel kick. The kid was a blur of motion, but Oz blocked each attack.

Jomtong came at him with a looping punch, and Oz caught his wrist with one hand and grabbed the inside of his thigh with the other. Then he picked Jomtong off the mat and slammed him to the ground. Oz rushed to follow it with a strike, but Lohr grabbed him and threw him to the corner of the ring.

"Get back!"

"But—"

"This is combat training, not professional wrestling."

Oz ducked under the top rope and onto the floor before storming off to the locker room, and that's when Colt noticed Agent Graves. He was standing in the doorway, his arms crossed. But he wasn't watching the fight. He was watching Colt.

CHAPTER 35

The energy drink started to wear off halfway through mathematics, an accelerated class that combined algebra, geometry, and trigonometry. Colt had been hoping he wouldn't have to take any of the classes they were stuck with back at Chandler High, but the cadets still had to learn the basics on top of all their other course work and the physical training.

Staying awake would have been difficult under any circumstance, but after a restless night in the rock hard bunk bed, it was impossible. Colt started to doze off when the door opened and Jomtong walked in, back from his trip to the infirmary. At first Colt had thought that Oz had broken his back, but Jomtong had just had the wind knocked out of him.

If mathematics was boring, chemistry was intolerable. The instructor actually wore a white lab coat with a pocket protector, and he spent the entire hour reading the syllabus word for word. Colt tried to follow along, but he ended up doodling for most of the class. It wasn't until the bell was about to ring that he noticed that the instructor only had four fingers on each hand, and two small horns jutting from a cloud of gray hair.

Things started looking up in fourth period. Basic Espionage was an entry-level course, but it was going to involve a lot of hands-on training. The instructor, Agent Huber, was a former CIA operative who had spent most of his career as a spy in Eastern Europe during the height of the Cold War. He had interesting stories, and according to the syllabus they were going to learn how to wiretap, forge documents, and turn household items into everything from weapons to bombs.

Lunchtime provided the first opportunity for Colt to tell Danielle about everything that happened the night before.

"Maybe we should tell someone," she said.

"Who?"

"What about Ms. Skoglund?"

"Let me know how that goes," Colt said as the bell rang.

He had been looking forward to Introduction to Flight all day. The classroom was inside the stadium, with a wall of windows that overlooked the aerial field where the cadets had been practicing hoverboard and jet pack maneuvers the night before.

As Colt and Danielle sat down, the door opened and Giru Ba walked in. Conversation stopped as the cadets watched her walk to the front of the room. She stood there, regarding them with her enormous eyes as though she was assessing their worthiness to be in the class.

"Welcome," she said, her voice melodic and rich. "I have been sent by Captain Starling to escort you to the aerial field. Please leave your computers in the classroom. You will not need them for the rest of our time together."

"Does that mean we're going to ride on those hoverboards today?" Pierce asked, betraying his excitement.

Giru Ba blinked as she regarded him. "There is that possibility," she said. "It will depend on your aptitude and sense of balance. Now please, follow me."

She led them through a series of corridors until they came to a tunnel that led to the field. Colt kept to the back of the group, hoping to avoid any kind of contact with her. He still didn't know what to think after everything that had happened the night before.

When they got to the field, the clouds had given way to sunlight for the first time since Colt had arrived in Virginia. Flags snapped in the wind as second-year cadets in gray uniforms zipped around the obstacles in jet packs, while their instructor barked commands.

"Welcome to Tesla Stadium," Giru Ba said. "This is where we will spend most of our time together. Your instructor, Captain Starling, is rather unorthodox, but his students achieve the highest marks year after year. Our hope is that you will do the same."

A rush of wind blew across the field as a figure on a hoverboard raced toward them. He was dressed in an instructor's black CHAOS uniform, but since he was wearing a full helmet with a tinted mask, nobody could see his face.

He pulled up in front of the cadets, his silver board bouncing up and down as though it were resting on the surface of the ocean. Below, two clusters of bright lights glowed like embers in a fire. Colt figured it was some kind of exhaust system, or maybe they held the electrical charge that repelled against the charge on the earth's surface. After all, that was supposed to be what kept the hoverboard afloat.

The instructor removed his helmet and shook his head before running a gloved hand through his thick blond hair. He was older than Colt had imagined—probably in his late forties—but he was still handsome despite the extra twenty pounds that made his face look slightly bloated.

"Good afternoon. My name is Captain James Starling," he said, flashing a perfect smile that shone unnaturally white. From the way he stood—his head cocked back, one hand on his hip, and the other cradling his helmet—there was no doubt that he spent a good deal of time looking at himself in the mirror.

"Be a dear and hold on to this for me, will you?" He knelt down and handed his helmet to Stacy, who wasn't given the opportunity to refuse. "I'd like to welcome you to Introduction to Flight, one of the most anticipated classes in the entire academy." He stopped when the ground started to shake. An enormous transport vehicle with six wheels rumbled toward them. It was gray, with a CHAOS insignia stretched across the hood.

"Excellent timing," he said.

Colt could feel the rumble of its engine reverberating in his chest. The driver was actually a service bot that looked a lot like the SVC-9 unit that had shaved Colt's head, except it was wearing coveralls and a trucker cap. It walked over and opened the back hatch, revealing rack after rack of hoverboards.

"If you'd be so kind as to form a single-file line, our mechanical friend will hand each of you a helmet and a hoverboard."

Pierce was first, though to Colt's surprise, Stacy was actually second. She had dropped Captain Starling's helmet and pushed her way through the group, nearly knocking over a male cadet who was twice her size.

"Patience, please. There are plenty of hoverboards for everyone," Captain Starling said, chuckling as though amused by the enthusiasm.

The line moved quickly, and before long Colt had strapped on a helmet and was holding a silver hoverboard that shone like a newly polished bumper.

"Very good," Captain Starling said once everyone was properly equipped. "We have enough time that each of you should get at least one run around the track, and possibly a second. But before we start, let's go over some of the basics, shall we?"

Giru Ba demonstrated the proper mounting technique, showing them everything from where to find the ignition switch to which foot should go in the front binding and which in the back. When she was done, Colt pressed his ignition key and his hoverboard fired up, lifting about a foot off the ground. He placed his left foot in the front binding and his right foot in the back. Somehow the board sensed that he was in position, and the straps tightened on their own.

He stood there for a moment, arms held wide as he tried to find his balance. It was similar to a surfboard, but it was still different—more sensitive—and he could feel the power surging beneath him.

"For those of you who have managed to stay on your feet, the remote control in your hand is more than an ignition switch—it's also your throttle," Captain Starling said. "If you drop it, there's a kill switch behind your back foot."

Colt looked around, but there were only a handful of other cadets standing on their hoverboards—Jomtong, Stacy, Grey, Bar-Ryak, and a girl named Olivia who had been on the U.S. gymnastics team. Everyone else was struggling to various degrees. Some were able to get both feet on the board, but they'd fall off after a few seconds. Others—like Danielle—were completely lost. Captain Starling and Giru Ba did their best to help, but it was clear that not everyone was going to get a shot at the track today.

"This is infuriating!" Danielle had tumbled face-first into a patch of snow. There was a red blotch on her cheek, and several strands of hair had fallen loose from her ponytail only to get caught in her mouth.

"You're trying too hard," Colt said. "Just relax, bend your knees, and—"

"Save it!"

"He's right, you know," Captain Starling said as he offered a hand to help her up. "I want you to take your time and imagine that you're simply standing on the ground." He continued to hold her hand as she placed her left foot on the board and then her right. "There you are," he said. "You've got it."

No sooner had he pulled his hand away than Danielle started to teeter. She arched her back, trying to maintain her balance, but she overcompensated and ended up in the snow again.

"Stay at it," Captain Starling said. "You'll be an expert in no time."

"Yeah, right."

Captain Starling was about to walk past Colt when he stopped. "I know you from somewhere, don't I."

Danielle rolled her eyes. "He's Murdoch McAlister's grandson. You know, as in the Phantom Flyer."

"Of course!" He took Colt's hand and shook it vigorously, nearly pulling him off his hoverboard. "Why, you're an old pro at this flying thing, aren't you? How would you feel about taking the first lap around the course—you know, to show the other cadets how it's done."

"Sure. I guess," Colt said.

"Wonderful!" Captain Starling turned around to face the other cadets. "If I can have your attention, it looks like we have a special treat today. I've just learned that a descendant of the Phantom Flyer himself is a part of our class, and I've asked him to take the first lap. So without further ado, I present . . ." His face went blank, as though he had just been struck with a bout of amnesia. "I'm sorry," he said, leaning over to whisper into Colt's ear. "But I'm afraid I didn't catch your first name."

"It's Colt."

"Of course. Colt McAlister!" Captain Starling said with a wink. "Go on then. The stage is yours."

Colt pressed the throttle harder than he intended and the board shot forward, nearly knocking him over. Somehow he kept his balance, but he was headed toward a pillar that was part of an obstacle course. Instinct took over, and Colt leaned to the right until his body was nearly parallel with the ground. The board cut hard, following his movement, and he shot around the pillar and headed for the track.

"Nicely done!" Captain Starling shouted.

It didn't take long for Colt to get the hang of things. He zipped around the track like it was second nature, and in a way it was. He'd spent his entire life surfing and snowboarding, and the hoverboard was basically a combination of the two.

As he cruised around the last turn, Colt felt the hairs stand on the back of his neck. His eyes scanned the field, but he didn't see Heinrich Krone anywhere. Then he spotted him. He was standing in the stadium bleachers, but instead of his dark suit and driving cap, he was wearing a janitorial uniform as he pushed a broom.

Krone smiled, and Colt felt his stomach drop. He glanced back at the track to make sure that he wasn't going to veer off course, but when he looked back, Krone was gone. He'd been replaced by an old man with jowls and a thick mustache that hung over his top lip.

:: CHAPTER 36 ::

By Friday, Danielle had found a way to access the Internet. It was against school policy, but there was an unspoken rule that students in the information security program were expected to try as part of their training, and she was the first in her class to succeed.

She had been using it to track news for updates about their accident. At least one person claimed to have seen the man in the Mercedes pull out a gun and aim it at the driver of the white van. The testimony was corroborated when crime scene investigators found a Walther P99 on the side of the road.

Authorities claimed that the gun belonged to Heinrich Krone, who was in a coma and under twenty-four-hour police surveillance. If that was true, Colt wondered, then whom had he seen walking across campus with Agent Graves the other night, and who was that standing in the stadium during flight class?

Unfortunately someone had managed to get a picture of Ms. Skoglund's license plate with a camera phone, but by the time investigators had an opportunity to look it up, she had already broken into the Virginia Department of Transportation's database and changed the owner of the vehicle to a man by the name of Delbert Landgren, a retired hog farmer from Shickley, Nebraska. His place of residence was the Alexandria National Cemetery. After all, he had been dead for nearly twenty-five years.

Back home, Friday night usually meant going out with friends to a football game and then grabbing a pizza or some hamburgers. At the CHAOS Military Academy, the cadets used Friday night to catch up on homework. Danielle asked Colt to meet her in the Agricultural Records Room on the third floor of the library. It wasn't the most exciting backdrop for a Friday night, but since he had to do some research on a paper for Basic Espionage, he agreed.

The building reminded Colt of the New York City Public Library. It was constructed from enormous stone blocks, with pillars, archways, and ornate window frames. There were even lion statues lining the front steps. Inside, long corridors led to a myriad of rooms that were dedicated to more than just books. There were art galleries, an aviary, map chambers, a robotics lab, solarium, genealogy databases, and a host of study rooms, just to name a few.

Though it took him almost twenty minutes of searching, he eventually found the records room. It was in the far corner next to a stairwell. The door was closed but unlocked, and when he pushed it open the hinges creaked.

The room wasn't large, about the size of a convenience store, or maybe even a bit smaller. Most of the room was filled with filing cabinets, which would have made things feel cramped if it weren't for the vaulted ceilings and the wide windows that stretched along each wall, offering a fantastic view of the campus.

"You're late," Danielle said without looking up.

"It wasn't the easiest place to find," Colt said as he shut the door.

"That's kind of the point." She was seated at a long table with her back to the door, reading something on the monitor of her computer.

He walked over and set his backpack on a chair before he sat down. "So how did you manage to get online?"

"It's easier than you think," she said. "All of the buildings are lined with something called Tempest shielding, which is a kind of electromagnetic protection that keeps the bad guys from accessing data. It also keeps us from tapping into any outside wireless networks. But as long as I have enough windows and my microwave tech wireless card, all I need to do is point the antenna at the satellite and I can log onto the Internet whenever I want."

"Won't someone notice the activity?"

"I doubt it. Most Wi-Fi connections are omni-directional, but going microwave allows me to point at a satellite. Someone would have to be looking for the signal to see it, and if they don't know exactly where it is, it's like trying to find a needle in a haystack."

"So how did you sneak the wireless card through security?"

"I slipped it into Ms. Skoglund's purse," Danielle said. "Apparently security didn't notice."

Colt watched as the antenna on Danielle's wireless card swiveled while it searched for the satellite. "Speaking of Ms. Skoglund, did you get a chance to talk to her yet?"

"I thought you didn't trust her."

"If you do, that's good enough for me."

"Good, because she gave me this." Danielle reached into her backpack and pulled out what looked like a piece of yellowed parchment. It was wrinkled, and the edges were bent, but as she unfolded it, Colt could see that it was actually a map.

"Is that the school?"

Danielle nodded. "Back in the 1830s, the president of the university was an abolitionist who got involved in the Underground Railroad. The tunnel that you fell into was part of a network that was built beneath the entire campus, and it was actually used by fugitive slaves who were escaping to the North."

"That's amazing," Colt said. The tunnels led between the buildings, and there was even one that connected to a boathouse next to the river. "Where'd she find the map?"

"Downstairs in the archives."

"And they just let her take it?"

Danielle shrugged before she folded the map and slipped it back into her backpack. "It's taken awhile, but we're finally building a more complete profile on Heinrich Krone." She pulled up a file on her computer. "We already knew that he enlisted in the German army, went through special ops training, and then went to work for Germany's federal intelligence service. After that, he went off the grid."

"What happened?"

"Ms. Skoglund thinks he was a spy, but we're not sure. We couldn't find anything for about a ten-year period, and then he showed up as the Chief Security Officer at Trident Biotech."

"Wait . . . what?" Colt felt dumbstruck as he tried to process what she just said.

"Somehow word leaked that Trident was developing agents that could be used in biochemical weapons—you know, stuff like viruses that could wipe out an entire population—and they wanted Krone to make sure everything was sealed up tight. One of the federal investigators was found in a shallow grave outside of Yuma. A week later Krone disappeared."

Colt's mind churned as he tried to understand what all of this meant. "Do you think he had something to do with what happened in Iowa?"

"Maybe," Danielle said. "Or maybe it's just a coincidence."

"So why is he working with Lobo?" Colt asked. "I mean, on one hand he's trying to exterminate humanity, but on the other hand he's working for the guy who's in charge of protecting us against the Thule invasion."

"Think about it," Danielle said. "Lobo wants you out of the picture because you're a threat to his job, but the Thule want to kill you because you might rise up and destroy them. Either way, both sides want the same thing. So if Lobo is going to pay him for what he was already going to do, why not take the money?"

The door creaked open, and Danielle's face went pale. "I thought you were at the gym."

"It's nice to see you too," Oz said. "I finished early, so I thought I'd see what you guys were up to."

"Nothing really," she said. "Just studying."

"With McAlister? Yeah, right. He's not exactly the studying type." He took a bite from an apple that he was holding and leaned against the doorframe. "So, who did my dad pay a small fortune to? Because if he's handing out money, I want in on it."

Danielle looked at Colt and then at the ground.

"What?" Oz asked.

"Look," Colt said, his voice sullen. "I don't really know how to say this, but we think your dad was involved in Senator Bishop's death."

"Yeah, right."

"It's true," Danielle said. "Someone found documents that link him to a hired killer."

"Is this some kind of joke? Because it's not funny."

Colt shook his head. "I wish it was. Senator Bishop was part of the oversight committee that threatened to cut funding if your dad didn't step down, and the DAA thinks that your dad hired a guy named Heinrich Krone to kill him."

"Is he serious?"

Danielle's eyes were filled with tears as she nodded.

"It's been going on for a while," Colt said. "There were at least five others, and it looks like he's not done."

"How do you know?"

"Because my name is on the list." Colt reached into a pouch on his backpack and pulled out a thumb drive. "You can see for yourself. It's here."

"I don't get it," Oz said as he ran his fingers through his hair. "Why didn't you come to me?"

"Because we didn't know if we could trust you."

CHAPTER 37

One minute Colt was convinced that Oz had nothing to do with Operation Nemesis, and the next he wasn't sure. Oz certainly looked upset when Colt confronted him about his father's alleged involvement, but it could have been an act.

Colt thought about asking for a transfer to a different dorm room, but that was bound to raise questions he wasn't ready to answer. Thankfully Oz didn't show up until just before curfew, and he was gone by the time Colt woke up Saturday morning.

Grey asked if Colt wanted to grab some breakfast in the mess hall, but he decided to head over to the aerial field instead. He wanted to clear his head, and if he couldn't surf, riding a hoverboard was the next best thing. It looked like it was going to be a warm day. The sun was out, the sky was clear, and most of the snow had melted, leaving patches of white scattered across the grass. He worked on some basic maneuvers, trying to get used to the feel of the board as he glided across the track.

It was getting close to lunchtime when Agent Starling showed up with Giru Ba. He was talking, she was listening, and Colt hoped they wouldn't notice him. "Nice bit of flying, but you may want to consider bending your knees and leaning forward just a bit," Agent Starling said. "It'll decrease wind resistance and increase speed."

"Thanks," Colt said, but before he could break away, Agent Starling started in about his boyhood admiration for the Phantom Flyer. "If it weren't for your grandfather, I would never have become a world class flight instructor."

"I'll be sure to let him know."

"That's very kind of you," Agent Starling said, his smile showing teeth that were both impossibly straight and eerily white. Giru Ba stood behind him without saying a word, her large eyes focused on Colt. He felt uncomfortable under her gaze, and he wondered if she had telepathy and whether or not there was a way to block people from reading one's mind.

"Look, I'm scheduled for combat simulation in twenty minutes, and I haven't eaten anything all day," Colt said, hoping that Agent Starling would take the hint.

"What a coincidence. We were talking about heading over to the mess hall, weren't we?"

Giru Ba nodded, though her eyes never left Colt.

"Would you care to join us?" Agent Starling asked.

"I'd love to," Colt said, trying to sound polite. "I really would, but I don't want to be late for my training session."

"Then off you go," Agent Starling said with a salute.

After a quick lunch that consisted of grilled chicken and an energy drink, Colt headed off to Combat Simulation. The training session was held in what looked like an abandoned warehouse. The windowless walls were painted a sterile white, and massive girders crisscrossed a ceiling that stood fifty feet above the concrete floor.

Nine other cadets were already in the room. Danielle was talking to Stacy and a girl Colt hadn't met. Jomtong was there, along with Bar-Ryak and a cadet named Kethan Sareen. He was small, with short hair and a quick smile. Pierce stood nearby, slouched with his arms crossed, while Oz was off to the side, whispering something to Grey.

"Welcome to Wonderland!"

Everyone looked up to see an observation deck where Agent Graves was standing next to a man with round goggles and a waxed mustache. He was short and a bit overweight, with stubble on his head and a cherubic face that made it almost impossible to tell how old he was.

"The name's Agent Daniel David O'Keefe, though most of the cadets like to call me the Gamemaster. You'll know why soon enough," he said with a light Irish brogue. "And this here is Agent Graves, who has asked to observe today's exercise."

Agent Graves nodded, and as his eyes fell on Colt, a thin smile crossed his lips.

"Now for the uneducated, you happen to be standing inside one of the most amazing inventions in the history of this fine world," Agent O'Keefe said.

The air started to shimmer, and a moment later the cadets were standing in a dense rain forest. But something was off. The leaves on the trees were iridescent blue, the sky was pink, and the branches were filled with featherless birds that were a kind of charcoal color. Their eyes were covered in cataracts, and they had wings like bats.

"Simulation training allows us to create unique environments using holograms, so we can put you through scenarios without risking your precious little lives. Right now you're standing in a jungle on the planet Bantoah," Agent O'Keefe said. "Go on, touch something." He stood with his hands on his hips, smiling as the cadets did as they were instructed. "The technology we developed gives dimension to the holograms. It feels real, doesn't it?"

The air shimmered again, and moments later they were standing in what looked like Times Square, only there were hovercars flying overhead and strange aliens walking the streets alongside human counterparts. The simulation was so real that Colt could smell a nauseating mixture of urine and exhaust as though it were real. Virtually every square inch of real estate was covered with some kind of advertisement. In fact, there was so much visual noise that it was practically impossible for any one message to stand out over the others.

Agent O'Keefe explained that the city would be the backdrop for their training exercise, and he offered no apologies for lifting it directly from the pages of a Phantom Flyer comic book. "In this scenario, your objective is to stop a crackpot robot that calls itself Intellitron from launching nuclear missiles. It wants to wipe out humans so a bunch of godless machines can take over."

"I thought this looked familiar," Colt said. "The Phantom Flyer got sucked through a rift and into an alternate Earth where a scientist was working on a new artificial intelligence program for the military," he said. "One of the robots he was testing turned on him. It's actually Intellitron's first appearance."

"Who didn't know that?" Danielle said, rolling her eyes.

Colt ignored the sarcasm. "It hacked into the Pentagon and sent something like a dozen nuclear warheads into Russia, which pretty much started World War III."

"So how do we stop him? Or it? Or whatever it is?"

"Let's hope we get lucky," Stacy said, butting into their conversation. "It has super intelligence, it can rip a tank in half, and you can't destroy it because it can repair itself."

As Agent O'Keefe went over some of the ground rules, Colt looked to the sky for caped superheroes. He didn't see any coming, but he noticed that Agent Graves was watching him.

"There's a building called the Omega Foundation just around the corner and down the block," Agent O'Keefe said as he went over their primary objective. "You have exactly forty-five minutes to break in and shut that robot down before it uploads the launch codes for those nukes. How you accomplish that objective is up to you."

He flipped a switch on what looked like some kind of remote control, and a cache of weapons and other supplies appeared. There was an FGM-148 Javelin anti-tank missile with a launcher, an M82A1 sniper rifle, three M4A1 assault rifles, an M60E3 machine gun, two Sig Sauer P228 handguns, a satchel with a computer, and four ammunition belts filled with Electro Magnetic Pulse grenades.

"Now remember," Agent O'Keefe said, "you're in a densely populated urban setting, and CHAOS has a zero tolerance policy when it comes to civilian casualties. This isn't a video game, and I don't want anyone to go in there with guns blazing. You're part of a covert mission, and your assignment is to eliminate a single target. So if you want to pass this test, make sure you keep that in mind. Oh, and I almost forgot," he added with the hint of a smile. "I thought you might have a bit of fun with this."

The air shimmered, and what looked like a fifteen-foot-tall robot made out of spare parts from a Sherman tank appeared in

the middle of the street. A cab driver slammed on his brakes and
veered over the curb and into a hydrant.

"This big galoot is what you call an ABS," Agent O'Keefe said.
"Does anyone besides Romero know what it stands for?"

Colt raised his hand. "Armored battle suit?"

"True enough," Agent O'Keefe said. "There's a cockpit inside
the chest where the driver sits." He looked down at the watch on
his wrist. "Time is ticking, so you better get to it."

:: CHAPTER 38 ::

A s the noise of the city blared around them, Pierce suggested that they assign a field commander to run the mission from the ground. He was quick to volunteer for the position.

"I think we should vote on it," Stacy said as a rickshaw pulled by a robot with a single wheel sped by.

Pierce sneered. "You heard him, we don't have time. If the clock runs out before we find that robot, we fail."

"I nominate Oz." The words spilled from Colt's mouth before he knew what he was saying. But he knew that despite the distance that had grown between them, it was the right choice. Oz had been training in simulators since he was old enough to hold a weapon, and Colt knew if they wanted to pass the test, they were going to need his experience.

"Any other nominees?" Stacy asked, but nobody said a word. "Okay then, all in favor of Oz?" Eight hands went up, leaving Pierce and Oz as the only dissenters.

Oz stood there looking confused, as though he had no idea why Colt had nominated him. "I guess that settles it," Stacy said. "So what's the plan?"

Oz hesitated as his eyes went from team member to team member. "Okay," he finally said. "If this scenario sticks to the script, Intellitron has control of the Omega Foundation. That means it's running the defense shields, repulsor rays, elevators, and even temperature control. We need to get Danielle close enough to tap into the operating system so she can shut that thing down before it launches the nukes."

"As soon as I break through one firewall, it'll build another," Danielle said. "I won't be able to type fast enough to keep up."

"You'll find a way, or we'll fail," Oz said.

"No pressure or anything."

Oz ignored her and turned to the rest of the group. "While she's launching a cyber attack, the rest of you are going to create a diversion."

"What are you going to do?" Pierce asked. "Sit back and take all the credit when we're done?"

"If you have a problem with me, we can settle it after class," Oz said. "But for now, we pass or fail as a team."

"Whatever."

"Excuse me?"

Pierce glared at him, his teeth grinding as he clenched his jaw. "Nothing."

"If anybody gets close enough to take Intellitron out, do it," Oz said, turning his attention to the rest of the group. "But don't take any crazy risks. We're starting with ten agents, and that's the number I want to see when we finish."

"Wait," Danielle said. "I thought we couldn't get hurt."

"That's not exactly true," Oz said. "But this is only a Level One scenario, which means the risk of injury is minimal. You can still be eliminated, though, so make sure you don't get hit with a kill shot."

He divided up the weapons and let Grey drive the ABS. Grey scrambled up the handrails and into the hatch as if he was worried that Oz might change his mind.

By the time the team arrived at the Omega Foundation, police had already set up a perimeter around the building, keeping the growing crowd at bay as best they could. The main entrance to the building was sealed, so Pierce suggested that they go through the sewers. Oz was quick to point out that they didn't have any schematics to know where the tunnels would lead, much less which would open up to the basement level. They did, however, have some heavy weapons.

The street rumbled as Grey moved the ABS into position, taking aim at the front door with a rocket launcher that was mounted on his right shoulder. With the flip of a switch, a rocket hissed before it slammed into the doors. Metal, brick, and glass erupted, and when the dust settled there was a gaping hole in the side of the building.

Pierce shook his head. "That was real subtle."

"Let's go!" Oz shouted. Bar-Ryak was the first inside, followed by Jomtong, Danielle, Stacy, and then Kethan.

The air filled with a strange buzzing sound. Colt looked up to see three robots with domed heads flying toward them. They were covered in armored casing, and they had organic wings, as though they had been grafted from a dragonfly the size of a rhinoceros. "Scarabs!" he yelled. He remembered them from the comic book, and if this scenario played out anything like the story, the cadets were in trouble.

Pierce raised his M4A1 assault rifle and was about to fire when Oz wrapped his hand around the barrel and ripped it away.

"Do you know what kind of armor those things have? Bullets

would bounce off them and into the crowd. Stop trying to be a hero and get inside!"

"But—"

"Now!"

Pierce hesitated, but Oz shoved the rifle into his chest and watched Pierce run into the building with the others.

The scarabs were part of the Omega Foundation's defense system, and they had been activated when the wall was breached. Waves of energy erupted from the palms of their hands. The blasts ripped into the sidewalk, sending clumps of asphalt into the air as the crowd screamed. Nervous police officers fired back, sending a hail of bullets into the sky, but they ricocheted off the scarabs just as Oz had predicted.

Colt's heart pounded as the scarabs drew closer, red eyes pulsing as wings pounded and flames shot out from the heels of their jet boots. He was about to head into the building when he spotted a kid with a hoverboard standing behind one of the barricades. Before the kid knew what was happening, Colt grabbed the board, slipped his feet into the bindings, and took off.

"Where're you going?" Oz shouted.

"To create a diversion!"

As Colt raced toward the scarabs, one raised a hand and took aim. At the last possible moment Colt leaned back, and the energy blast ripped through the air where his head had been just moments before. The bolt struck a building across the street, tearing away part of the façade. Someone screamed, and Grey swung the ABS around, moving it to shield a girl and her dog from debris the size of a Volkswagen Beetle. Concrete rained down, bringing the massive ABS to its knees, but Grey kept it from toppling over.

Colt banked hard and pulled an EMP grenade from a pouch

in his weapons belt as one of the scarabs reached for him. The grenade was magnetized, so when it came in contact with the robot's exoskeleton, it latched on. There was a flare of light as tendrils of energy spread across the scarab like tiny bolts of lightning. The machine convulsed. Its eye faded and its body went limp as it fell, landing on a garbage truck that buckled under the weight.

:: **CHAPTER 39** ::

C olt led the other scarabs down a four-lane street, weaving around flying buses and skirting hovercabs. He whizzed past drivers covered in scales and fur. Some had horns, and others had more eyes than he could count. One even had two heads, but there was no time to gawk—not with a pair of ten-ton killing machines chasing after him.

He knew that a moving target was more difficult to hit than something stationary, so he tried to change his elevation, diving below the flow of traffic and then shooting high above. He narrowly missed what looked like a 1962 Corvette, though the hovercar roared through the skyline without any wheels. The driver blared his horn as he cranked his steering wheel to the left. Momentum took the Corvette into oncoming traffic, but the driver managed to swerve back into his lane before he collided with a flying sanitation truck.

One of the scarabs sent an energy blast that missed Colt but hit an animated advertisement for an apparel store. The screen exploded in a shower of sparks that lit up the night like a burst of fireworks. Colt ducked, covering his face with his arms as glass pelted his uniform. The shards cut through fabric and nicked his skin. Simulation or not, he felt pain, and the blood looked real.

There was a break in the buildings, and he took a hard left, pulling in front of a delivery truck at the last second. The scarabs tried to follow, but the truck smashed into one of the machines, sending it reeling into the side of a building. There was an explosion, and people screamed as the scarab fell, ripping through an awning before it landed in a crumbled heap.

Its eyes faded, but Colt didn't stick around to see if it was going to get back up. He raced down an alley that felt like a narrow canyon. An occasional light flickered over a back door or in a random window, but it didn't help much. If it weren't for the glow beneath his hoverboard, he would have been flying blind.

For a moment the fragrance of oregano and basil overpowered the stench of garbage as he rushed past a man sweeping the back stoop of what must have been a restaurant. Colt hoped the red stains on the man's apron were marinara sauce, not blood. The sweeper looked confused when he saw Colt, but when he caught sight of the scarab he dropped his broom, ran inside, and slammed the door shut.

Colt was startled when something jumped from a stack of crates and into the shadows behind a garbage bin. His arms flailed as he tried to keep from falling off his hoverboard. The bindings held tight, and he managed to maintain his balance as his heart pounded and his breathing grew shallow. He looked over his shoulder and saw the red eye of the scarab pulsing in the darkness.

The machine raised both hands, and waves of energy shot from its palms, cutting through the darkness in jagged streaks. One blast hit a light pole, ripping it from the ground before it twirled through the alley and into a wall. The second grazed Colt's rib cage, singeing his uniform before it struck a rusted 1968 Plymouth Valiant. The impact lifted the car off the pavement, flipping it over before it landed upside down.

Metal crunched and glass shattered, but Colt kept going. He thought about ditching the hoverboard and trying to escape through one of the buildings, but he knew the scarab would follow. If any civilians inside got injured, points would be deducted, and Colt didn't want to be responsible for the team failing. Besides, escape was never an option. He was a decoy, which meant he needed to stay out in the open.

It was almost too late when Colt noticed that the alley was about to end. He banked hard to the left until he was practically parallel with the ground. His board scraped the brick wall and sparks flew before he straightened out and cut between two buildings. Moments later he was in a crouch, bursting back into the street.

"Sorry!" he shouted over his shoulder, after he narrowly missed a woman who was walking some kind of dog with a spiked tail and tusks. When he turned back around, he was staring at a billboard fixed to the back of a flatbed truck, and he was close enough to reach out and touch it. He managed to jump out of the way, but the scarab didn't have time to react. It burst through the sign and ripped it from the back of the vehicle.

The momentum threw the sign into a storefront across the street, and the truck rolled three times before it crashed into a fire hydrant that burst like a geyser.

Somehow the scarab kept coming.

Colt wondered if the team would get points deducted because of the wreck. He needed to get off the street and away from the crowds to avoid any more collateral damage, but he didn't know where to go.

Thanks to the police barricades, traffic had come to a standstill both on the skyway overhead and in the streets down below. Frustrated drivers blared their horns and shouted out their windows. One driver tried to make a U-turn, but he was sideswiped by a delivery truck.

The Omega Foundation loomed over the cityscape. Smoke poured from a shattered window at least twenty stories overhead, as well as from the gaping hole down near the entrance. Colt hoped that everything inside was going according to plan. He sped toward the building with the scarab right behind him, dodging and weaving through the vehicles.

The only weapons Colt had were the EMP grenades, and from that distance and at that speed, the odds of hitting the scarab weren't very good. Besides, if he missed, there was a chance that he could take out at least one hovercar, if not more.

Then he had an idea.

Colt raced toward the Omega Foundation, knees bent and head forward. The scarab fired again and blasts of energy slammed into random windows, sending a shower of glass to the empty sidewalk below. Jaw clenched and eyes focused, Colt kicked down with his back foot, and the nose of the hoverboard shot straight up. Instead of following the trajectory of the street, he was climbing the building.

The scarab gave chase.

Flames leapt out from a broken window overhead. Colt figured that Intellitron was holed up, but if his plan was going to work, he had to time it just right. He reached for one of the magnetic EMP grenades, set the timer, and let it fall from his fingers where it latched on to the metal frame of his hoverboard. The tiny green light flashed as it counted down to detonation.

Quick as he could, he fished out five more grenades and set them as well. He closed his eyes, took a deep breath, and hit the release button on his bindings. They unlatched, and Colt kicked hard. He dived through the open window as the first grenade detonated. There was a flash and an explosion of light and sound, setting off a chain reaction. The hoverboard sputtered and died, falling as waves of electricity leapt at the last scarab, engulfing it in crackling light. Its back arched and fingers twitched as its body started to convulse.

Air rushed from Colt's lungs as he hit the floor, flipping over backward. He crashed into a desk, sending papers flying like a swirl of confetti before he came to rest against the wall. Groaning, he opened his eyes and saw Intellitron.

:: CHAPTER 40 ::

ntellitron was taller than Oz, with a broad chest, narrow waist, and long arms that ended in four fingers. Its body was wrapped in alloy casing, and its eyes glowed an angry red as métal tentacles shot out from a compartment in its back. They writhed like cobras under a trance. One grabbed Jomtong, who dropped his Sig Sauer P228 as the robot slammed him into a table.

Colt barely had time to react as Intellitron threw an office chair that smashed into the wall over his head. He rolled out of the way, wincing as he landed behind a desk that was flipped over on its side. It wasn't much in the way of cover, but it was better than nothing.

His hand fell to his rib cage, and when he pulled it away, it was covered in blood. It didn't make sense. There wasn't supposed to be any risk of injury—at least not serious injury—but his side felt like it was on fire every time he took a breath. Colt hoped he hadn't broken a rib, but even if he had, he had to focus. The mission wasn't over.

Nearby, Danielle had her computer hardwired into the building's network. Her fingers danced across the keys as she tried to shut down the system before Intellitron launched any of the nuclear missiles. Oz stood over her, holding an M4A1 assault rifle, but the bullets were useless against the robot's armored shell.

"I can't break through," she said.

"Keep trying!" Oz discarded the rifle and picked up a rocket launcher, firing the FGM-148 Javelin anti-tank missile. It was designed to penetrate armor up to 60 mm thick, and it hissed as it sped toward the robot. Intellitron knocked it aside with one of its mechanical tentacles as though it were batting a fly with a newspaper. The missile exploded, blowing another hole in the building. The floor shook and walls swayed as a heavy wind whipped through the room, sending papers swirling.

"Your attempt to override my primary function is futile," the robot said, shooting a tentacle toward Oz. It picked him up and threw him against a wall, where he slumped to the floor.

Danielle's eyes were wide as another tentacle crashed down on her computer. Broken components flew in every direction as the same tentacle coiled around her arms, pinning them to her sides. She screamed, kicking her legs as she tried to break free. The robot held her in the air so that her face was mere inches from its glowing eyes. It regarded her for a moment, as though studying her at a molecular level. Then the tentacle moved toward the gaping hole.

Colt felt a wave of panic as instinct took over. More tentacles shot toward him, but time felt like it had slowed. He leapt out of the way of one and then another before wrapping his hands around the tentacle that held Danielle. Sparks flew as he ripped it from the machine's back. It released its grip, sending Danielle rolling across the floor.

Intellitron lashed out at Colt, and tentacles whipped across his face and chest, cutting into his skin. It grabbed him by the shoulders and drove its metal forehead into his nose. Blood splattered across the front of Colt's uniform like crimson raindrops as another tentacle wrapped around his ankles. Before he realized what had happened, he was dangling upside down.

There was a series of sounds like metal hitting metal, and Colt looked up to see five EMP grenades latched on to Intellitron's body. There was an explosion followed by a blinding flash as electricity pulsed across the robot.

Colt fell on his head as the machine staggered to a keyboard, where it started to type faster than Colt could track. "Initiating launch sequence," it said in a synthesized voice.

Colt rose to his feet, his head swimming as he tried to maintain his balance. The cadets didn't have enough firepower to stop Intellitron. Not knowing what else to do, he launched at the machine. Like a linebacker, he wrapped his arms around its waist and drove with his legs, heading straight for the gap in the wall.

"No!" Danielle cried out, but it was too late. Colt jumped off the ledge.

As it fell, the robot tried to latch on to the wall, but the bricks crumbled. Colt thought about closing his eyes and waiting for the simulation to fade, but he had a nagging suspicion that if he died inside the scenario he was really going to die.

He drove his elbow into Intellitron's chest and pushed off with his hands, trying to create separation so he could get a better view of his surroundings. They were about thirty feet above a crowded skyway filled with hovercraft, and they were closing fast. Traffic was backed up for blocks, and just below a semi tractor-trailer was stuck behind a hovercycle with a sidecar. It rumbled in idle as smoke poured from its exhaust pipes.

Twenty feet.

Colt glanced up and saw the other cadets watching from high above, the wind tousling their hair as they stood in the gap.

Ten feet.

The trailer was close enough that Colt could see the rust spots and scratches. He braced for impact, and with a thud his chest hit the truck. Oxygen exploded from his lungs, and if his ribs weren't broken before, he was fairly certain they were now. His fingernails scraped across the paint as momentum took him over the edge, but somehow he managed to hold on.

As he dangled over the side of the trailer, Colt felt something latch on to his ankle. He looked down to see Intellitron hanging on by one of its mechanical tentacles. The machine was heavy, and Colt's grasp started to slip. He tried to kick free, but a second tentacle grabbed him around the waist as a third took hold of his arm. The robot pulled itself up, trying to climb over him like a spider.

Colt looked down and saw a fire truck speeding toward them, lights flashing as it tore through the sky. He counted to three and let go.

:: CHAPTER 41 ::

The atmosphere shimmered before it disappeared, replaced by the sterile white of the simulation room. The sudden shift back to reality was disorienting, as the frenzied sounds of the city were replaced by the soft hum of air rushing through the vents overhead.

Colt's heart pounded and his hands shook as they ran over his ribs. His side was tender to the touch, and the blood that stained his uniform was warm and sticky. He wondered if Agent O'Keefe had lied to them about the danger, or if there had been some kind of mix-up when the instructor programmed the simulation. Either way, thanks to Colt's fall, the simple act of breathing had become painful.

As he looked up, Colt noticed that the other cadets were staring at him. "What?" he said.

"You're one of them, aren't you?" Pierce asked, stepping forward. It was more of an accusation than a question. "I mean, it's either that or you're some kind of freak mutant. Nobody could do what you did in that simulation."

Colt's heart raced. "What are you talking about?"

"Don't play stupid," Pierce said. "My dad warned me that shapeshifters would try and infiltrate this place, and he was right."

"Whatever." Colt fought the urge to run. What if the meta-morphosis had begun? Had his skin been replaced by green scales? Were his eyes glowing? He was desperate for a mirror, but he stood there unmoving, trying to play it cool.

"Then how did you tear the tentacle off that thing?" Pierce asked. "And how did you survive jumping out of a skyscraper without a parachute?"

Colt relaxed, though just a little. If there had been a physical change, Pierce would have mentioned that first. "It's called luck," he said. "Or maybe it was adrenaline. How do I know? I just reacted."

"Liars won't look you in the eye, and they get sarcastic," Pierce said. "You know, to try and throw you off."

Colt made a point of looking Pierce directly in the eye. "What, so now you're an interrogation expert too? I'm surprised they haven't given you Lobo's job already."

Everyone laughed.

"All you're doing is proving my point," Pierce said as his face flushed red.

"What's wrong with you?" Danielle asked. "Besides the fact that you're obviously jealous."

"Of him? Yeah, right."

"Be careful," Colt said. "You didn't look her in the eye. And you have to admit, it was kind of sarcastic."

There was more laughter as Pierce clenched his hands. "Don't try and flip this around, McAlister. You're not going to think it's funny when the Depart of Alien Affairs shows up and takes you away in handcuffs."

Pierce's father was on the Senate Committee on Intelligence, which oversaw the DAA, but Colt doubted that Pierce had that kind of pull. Still, the idea of being led out of the academy in handcuffs was unnerving.

"If Colt was a shapeshifter, then why did he fight against the Thule back in Arizona?" Danielle said. "That doesn't make any sense."

"How am I supposed to know? Maybe it was a setup."

"I didn't think it was possible, but maybe you really are as dumb as you look," Oz said, surprising Colt by coming to his defense.

"Then how do you explain what he did?" Pierce asked. "I mean, there was no way we were going to beat that scenario, and then Colt shows up and takes out Intellitron with his bare hands? Give me a break. He's one of them."

"Have you actually seen a shapeshifter up close?" Oz asked. "Not a picture, but in the flesh?"

"It doesn't matter."

"That's what I thought. What color is their blood?"

"Everybody knows that," Pierce said. "It's green."

"And what color is his blood?" Oz nodded toward Colt, who had bloodstains all over his uniform.

"That's just some kind of trick," Pierce said.

The door to the observation deck opened, and Agent O'Keefe came running down the staircase, his round face a deep shade of red as his boots pounded the steps. Agent Graves was nowhere to be seen. "Is everyone okay?" He was breathing heavily and dabbing a handkerchief across his brow. "I'm not sure what happened, but . . ." His voice trailed off when he saw Colt. "Oh my."

"It looks worse than it feels," Colt said, though he couldn't help wincing.

"This is O'Keefe," the agent said, speaking into the communicator on his wrist. "We need a medibot in simulation room four, and we need it now!"

"Really, I'm fine."

"Nonsense," Agent O'Keefe said. "Now let me take a look at that."

Colt raised his arm to show him the gash across his ribs.

"In all my years, nothing like this has ever happened," Agent O'Keefe said. "I swear on the Holy Bible that I programmed a Level One scenario, but somehow it ran at Level Three. I don't know what went wrong."

Colt's first thought was that Krone had broken into the system and changed the settings, just as he'd done with that robot back at Oz's house.

The doors to the simulation room opened, and a white robot with a red cross on its chest plate rolled in. It was squat, with a perfectly square body, a flat head, long arms with delicate fingers, and track wheels like a miniature tank.

"Over here," Agent O'Keefe said, waving his thick arm. "As for the rest of you, you're dismissed."

Pierce hesitated before he moved close enough that Colt could hear him whisper. "This isn't over . . . not by a long shot."

:: CHAPTER 42 ::

It was more than an hour before Colt was allowed to leave the training facility. The medibot made him strip to his boxer briefs, which wasn't as easy as it should have been. His uniform had fused with the skin around his rib cage, and it burned as he peeled the fabric away.

"There's a good lad," Agent O'Keefe said, watching Colt wince as the medibot dabbed at his wounds with rubbing alcohol. When it was done, the machine patched him up with some gauze and medical tape before it went through a series of tests, checking his blood pressure, heart rate, and reflexes. Then it ran an X-ray. There were no broken ribs, but they were bruised, and according to the report it left, they were going to take at least three weeks to heal.

"I don't know what happened, but we'll get to the bottom of this," Agent O'Keefe said as he handed Colt a fresh uniform. "In the meantime, if you need anything, you know where to find me."

"Thanks," Colt said.

"And don't you worry about that Bowen boy. Pierce, is it? He's all bark and no bite, if you catch my meaning." Agent O'Keefe winked before he took the stairs back up to the observation deck. A team of investigators had already assembled inside. Colt thought that he could see Ms. Skoglund, but she disappeared behind a wall before he could be sure.

〰〰〰〰〰〰〰〰〰〰〰〰

It wasn't quite five o'clock, but the lights that lined the walkways had already flared to life, creating a warm glow against the drab gray of twilight. What was left of the sun remained buried behind a bank of clouds, and from the look of things, they were destined to erupt with another winter storm.

Colt thought about going to the library so he could study, but he decided to head back to his dorm instead. He wanted to be alone so he could process everything that happened in the training scenario. Besides, the medibot had given him some pain medication and it was making him drowsy. He figured a quick nap before dinner might do him some good.

As he walked, he looked at his hands, wondering how long it would take before he started to show physical signs that he was turning into an alien. Who would be his friend when his body was covered in green scales? He supposed that turning into a genetic freak was a small price to pay if that's what it took to save the world.

"There you are!"

Colt turned around to see Danielle walking across the lawn. Her ears and nose were red from the cold, and he could see her breath streaming from her lips. "I tried to wait in the hall, but a security guard told me I had to leave," she said. "Are you okay?"

Colt shrugged. "My ribs are a little sore, but they gave me some pills that are supposed to help with the pain."

"I'm sorry about what happened with Pierce." She removed a strand of hair from her eyes. "He's such a jerk."

"It's no big deal," Colt said. "Besides, I've been thinking . . . maybe he's right."

"Are you serious?"

"What if I wake up tomorrow and I'm a full-blown monster?"

"But you controlled it in the simulation room, right?"

"Kind of," Colt said. "Something inside of me snapped, and I just reacted."

"You saved my life."

"It was only a simulation."

"A Level Three simulation," she said, correcting him. "If Intellitron had thrown me off the ledge, I would have been killed."

"Then I guess turning into a freak is already paying off."

Danielle went to hug him, but before he realized what had happened, she stabbed him in the neck with a syringe.

"Dani . . . wha . . . ?" His fingers started to tingle, and his lips grew heavy, like they were made of rubber. He tried to speak, but he couldn't form a coherent thought, much less make his jaw move. What had she done? His body started to sway, and then his knees gave out. He wanted to stand, to call for help, but he couldn't move. Then everything went black.

:: CHAPTER 43 ::

olt woke up in a strange bed feeling nauseous and disori-ented. His skin ached, he had the chills, and his forehead was covered in sweat. He tried to sit up, but the sudden movement was more than he could handle.

He closed his eyes and reached into his brittle memory, trying to piece together how he got there. The fragments were disjointed, but after he left the training center he ran into Danielle. They talked and then . . . Colt's hand went to his neck. Had she stuck him with a needle, or was that just a dream?

His mind was in a fog as he peeled back the comforter, took a deep breath, and slowly sat up. There was a draft in the room, and all he had on was a pair of boxers. Someone had set some socks and blue jeans and a long-sleeved T-shirt on the dresser, along with a pair of tennis shoes at the foot of the bed.

Arms shaking, he tried to steady himself against the mattress. He noticed a spot of blood that had seeped through the gauze taped to his ribs. Another wave of nausea rolled through him as he stood.

He had no idea what time it was, much less the day. For all he knew, he'd been unconscious for a week. There wasn't any mirror, but he could feel that his lips were cracked, as though he hadn't had anything to drink for some time.

He peered through the slats on the blinds; it was dark outside. There was a wide lawn, and beyond that a cluster of trees that would offer decent cover if he could make it that far without getting spotted. Then he saw two men not more than ten feet away, wearing armored vests and carrying M4 Carbine assault rifles. It was hard to tell from a distance, but he thought they were CHAOS agents.

He stepped away from the window and shook his head, trying to remember anything that would give him a clue as to what was going on. He was certain that he had run into Danielle, but why would she have drugged him? Maybe Lobo had threatened her family . . . or maybe she had been working with him all along.

The thought left him feeling empty. His parents were dead. His brothers were scattered across the globe. There was a chance that his best friend was part of a conspiracy to kill him, and his own grandfather hadn't told him that the government had shot him up with blood from a dead alien. If he couldn't trust Danielle, he didn't have anyone left.

His frustration was quickly turning to panic, so he closed his eyes and tried to focus. The medallion Grandpa had given him still hung around his neck, and he took it in his hand and read the inscription. If Colt had ever needed a refuge and strength in times of trouble, it was now, and he breathed a prayer.

There was movement outside the room. Heart pounding, he counted to a hundred and then slipped into the jeans and pulled the shirt over his head. The shoes were a perfect fit, and he laced them up, then walked over and placed his ear against the door.

There were muffled voices, but he couldn't tell how many people were out there, much less who they were.

He looked around for some kind of weapon and settled on a lamp. He removed the shade and unplugged it from the wall, wrapping the cord around the base before he held it like a club. It wasn't going to help much if whoever was out there had a gun, but it was better than nothing.

Taking a deep breath, he turned the brass knob. As the door clicked open, the hinges squeaked, stealing the advantage of surprise as he stepped into the empty hallway. The floorboards groaned as he crept toward the voices, but he made it to the end of the hallway without being spotted. It led to a small kitchen where a pot of coffee brewed on the countertop next to a gas stove. The strong smell made his stomach churn as he looked for a knife set or even a frying pan.

He caught movement out of the corner of his eye, and just managed to pull back before a tall man with broad shoulders and silver hair walked into the kitchen and poured himself a cup of coffee. The drugstore aftershave gave him away.

"Grandpa?"

The man hesitated before he turned around, coffee cup in hand. "It's good to see you up and about," he said, smiling before he took a sip.

Caught somewhere between relief and confusion, Colt struggled to process the flood of questions that bounced inside his head like ping-pong balls in a lottery machine.

"Is he awake?"

Colt felt his heart slam inside his chest when Danielle walked into the room. She had been smiling, but when she saw the look on his face her smile disappeared, replaced by something that resembled guilt, or maybe it was sadness. She started to say some-thing, but then she stopped and looked at Grandpa.

"What's going on?" Colt asked, his brows furrowed and his tone accusatory. "The last thing I remember is you jamming a syringe in my neck. Then I wake up who knows where with armed guards outside my window, I'm sick to my stomach, and I can barely stand up without falling over."

Grandpa looked down at the lamp that Colt still gripped in his hand. "I know things are a little confusing right now, but—"

"A little? I don't even know what's real anymore. My whole life has turned into one gigantic nightmare."

"It wasn't me," Danielle said, her voice timid as she looked at Colt with hopeful eyes. "I know what you saw, but I never would have done anything like that to you."

"Then I must have been hallucinating," Colt said. "Or maybe it was your evil twin from some kind of twisted alternate dimension."

"The person who attacked you may have looked like Danielle, but from what we can gather, it was Krone," Grandpa said. "He apparently shifted into her form before he injected you with the virus. That's why you're feeling under the weather."

The virus? Colt touched his neck where the needle had punc-tured his skin. As far as he knew, anyone who contracted it had died within forty-eight hours. Their skin would break out with boils and then their heart and lungs would shut down.

"I know what you're thinking, but you can relax," Grandpa said, a soft smile playing on his lips. "They finally got around to developing an antiserum, and from what we've been told it did the trick. You might not feel up to snuff for a day or two, but you're going to live."

Colt felt the tension subside, if only a little. "So where are we?"

"Faculty housing," Grandpa said. "I took a red-eye and got in early this morning. They had you in the infirmary, but I thought it might be more comfortable here. And it's about the closest thing to privacy we're going to find."

"How long was I out?"

"Oz found you last night," Danielle said.

"Oz?"

"When you didn't show up for dinner, he went looking for you," she said. "You were behind the chapel, out by the cemetery, and he carried you all the way to the infirmary."

"Where is he now?" Colt was confused. If Oz had been taking part in Operation Nemesis, then why would he have bothered doing something like that?

"He wasn't sure if you'd want to see him, so he went to the gym," Danielle said. "Anyway, the whole campus is freaking out. I mean, there's no way that anyone should have been able to get past security—even a shapeshifter. And now Pierce and a bunch of his friends are refusing to the leave their dorm rooms until everyone gets their blood tested again. Someone said that his dad is going to launch an investigation. Can you believe that?"

"If you're up to it, we need to talk," Grandpa said as he led them to a small living area. "It's time you met a few of the conspirators who have been looking out for you."

"Greetings," Giru Ba said. She was seated at a high-back chair next to a fireplace, her long fingers interlocked as they rested on her lap. Ms. Skoglund was there as well, nursing a cup of hot cocoa with a mound of whipped cream while Agent O'Keefe stood next to the window, looking out at the front lawn.

"I can see that you're confused, which is only natural," the alien said, her voice calm and melodic. "But if you'll allow me to explain—"

"Who are you?" Colt asked.

"A fair question," she said. "I'm an undercover agent working for the DAA, and I was given the task of earning Lobo's trust."

"Then you know about Operation Nemesis."

She nodded.

"So why haven't you arrested him?" Colt asked. "I mean, if you're in his inner circle, hasn't he mentioned anything about murdering his rivals?"

"I'm afraid not," she said. "He's rather paranoid at the moment, as I'm sure you understand. He considers me a trusted colleague, but his trust only goes so far."

"But you want us to trust you, is that it?"

"That's enough," Grandpa said.

"It's a fair question," Giru Ba said. "Trust is something that is earned, not freely given. And I understand your reservations."

Colt looked around the room, wondering if he could trust any of them. When his eyes fell on Danielle, her shoulders were slumped and her head was down. "I know it wasn't you," he said.

She looked up at him, confused.

"With the syringe . . . it wasn't you."

Danielle's lips curled into the slightest smile. "Do you want something to drink? There's some root beer in the fridge."

"I'm okay."

"I for one want to know what we're going to do about Lobo and his killer," Agent O'Keefe said. "The real reason we haven't arrested him is because all we have is circumstantial evidence. That man is a slippery one, and if we charged him now, his lawyers would have the charges dismissed before the case went to trial."

"What kind of evidence do we need?" Colt asked.

Agent O'Keefe didn't hesitate. "A confession."

"Then I'll get one."

"And how do you propose to do that? We've been trying to build a case against him for over a year, and we don't have anything."

"We set a trap that he can't resist."

"And what do you propose to use as the bait?"

"Me."

:: CHAPTER 44 ::

At first Oz didn't want to play any part in the scheme, and Colt felt guilty asking a son to turn against his father. But as Danielle said, "How else will you know if your dad is innocent?"

Oz reluctantly agreed.

They needed to lure Lobo to a site they could control, and so far everything had gone according to plan. Oz told his dad that Colt was meeting with an instructor who had been working with the Department of Alien Affairs, and he thought it had something to do with a shapeshifter having infiltrated the campus. The meeting was supposed to take place at midnight in a dilapidated barn that used to be part of the school's animal sciences program back when it was a university. When Lobo pressed for details, Oz said he didn't have any, but that he'd overheard Danielle and Colt talking while they were studying in the library.

Once everything was set in motion, Danielle worked with Agent O'Keefe and Ms. Skoglund to set up a network of wireless cameras and microphones inside the barn. The hope was that Lobo would be lulled into a false sense of comfort and confess to Operation Nemesis. He might not have pulled the trigger or poisoned anyone directly, but at the very least he was guilty of conspiracy to commit five murders, and attempting a sixth.

To keep Lobo from bolting, they needed someone to play the part of Colt's contact at the academy, and after a heated debate they settled on Ms. Skoglund. Agent O'Keefe and Giru Ba both volunteered, and Grandpa said that Lohr was willing to do whatever they asked, but Ms. Skoglund pointed out that she would be the least threatening of the group. They needed Lobo to feel confident or he was going to run.

"Besides," she said, "if anything goes wrong, the cavalry will be waiting in the wings to rescue us, right?"

Once that was settled, Giru Ba was assigned a team of two dozen DAA agents who would be waiting with Grandpa just out of sight, ready to storm the building and arrest Lobo once his confession had been recorded. There would also be a sniper with a clear line of sight to a bank of windows on the side of the barn. Grandpa wanted him there as a precaution, but Colt made sure the sniper was armed with tranquilizer darts instead of bullets. He knew what it was like to lose a parent, and he didn't want Oz to go through the same thing.

Colt spent the day holed up in Grandpa's apartment, trying to plan contingencies for every possibility. What if Lobo didn't show up? What if he spotted one of the DAA agents? What if he tried to take Colt to a new location? What if something happened to Ms. Skoglund?

"She knows the risk," Grandpa said. "We all do."

"But I don't want anyone to risk their life for me."

"This isn't about you, it's about doing whatever it takes to get the job done. Besides, I don't think you have much to worry about. She's a resourceful one."

"I hope you're right."

Colt baked a frozen pizza and distracted himself with a stack of comic books Grandpa had brought from home. As he flipped through the pages, he watched time and again how the Phantom Flyer overcame the odds to defeat villains that should have destroyed him. He wondered if he would be able to do the same.

As the night went on, Colt felt like a Thoroughbred horse stuck behind a gate, waiting for his race to start. Somehow he was frustrated, terrified and excited all at the same time. Then the clock finally struck eleven thirty and it was time to go.

It was cold out, but the sky was clear, and he could see the stars shining overhead as he cut through a patch of trees that skirted the cemetery behind the chapel. Thanks to a schedule that Ms. Skoglund found on one of the servers, Colt knew where the security detail would be stationed, and when. The last thing he needed was to get caught outside after curfew and blow the entire operation.

Colt wore a ballistic vest beneath a hooded sweatshirt, but Giru Ba had also given him a jacket that was constructed from the same nanotechnology used to make his cadet uniform. It was warm, but it also had hidden pockets that held some useful gadgets, just in case he ran into trouble. There was a set of Bola Cuffs that came in a metal disc about the size of a hockey puck. All he had to do was throw it, and four lengths of rope made with polyethylene fibers would eject and wrap around his target, effectively tying the person up. Each strand was as strong as a steel cable, but much thinner, and they only weighed about a tenth as much.

He also had a high lumen LED flashlight that didn't require

batteries. Instead, it used electromagnetic induction, which had something to do with magnetic fields and conductors, although Colt couldn't remember the specifics of how it worked.

The strangest gadget of the three was something called concrete foam, which came in what looked like miniature whipped cream cans, complete with red nozzles. Inside was a chemical compound that produced rapidly expanding foam that looked a bit like cement when it hardened. Colt wasn't sure how useful it was going to be, but it was there in case he needed it.

The enormous barn was nestled against a bank of trees that overlooked the Potomac River. From a distance it looked like the subject of a postcard, but as he got closer he could see the damage from years of neglect. The white paint was faded and peeling, casting the barn in a dull gray. Wide swaths of shingles were missing, and one of the doors that opened to the loft hung at an odd angle, threatening to fall at any time.

"All right, I'm here," Colt said, wondering if the tiny two-way radio transceiver implanted inside his auditory canal would really work.

"I know, I can see you," Danielle's voice said in his ear. She was back at Ms. Skoglund's apartment, where she sat in front of nine monitors that hung from the wall like oversized picture frames. One of the screens was a map of the school grounds, where a tracking device that doubled as Colt's belt buckle allowed them to see where he was at all times.

"How do I look?"

"Right now, you're just a little red dot on my screen. But once you're inside, we'll have full audio and video feeds."

He crossed the field and entered the barn through a side door that creaked as it opened. The sound triggered a flutter of activity, and when he shined his flashlight into the rafters he saw a colony of bats swarming overhead. Eventually he found a light switch that triggered a single bulb. It was feeble, but at least he could see where he was going.

It had been years since any animals had been stabled inside the barn, but Colt could still smell the faint scent of manure as he walked past three empty stalls. On the other side of the aisle was a tack room, but outside of a rusted lawnmower and workbench with an old Philips radio, it was empty. Next to that was a storage area, where an array of farm implements hung from the walls. Someone had managed to park a 1952 Ford Country Squire inside, which didn't leave much room for anything else. The tires were flat and it was buried under a thick layer of dust, but there were no dents, and the wood paneling that ran along the doors and fenders looked like it was in perfect condition.

Colt glanced at his watch. Three minutes to midnight. Suddenly he felt nervous. Getting Lobo to confess about his involvement in Operation Nemesis had seemed like a simple thing when he was in a room full of people, but now that he was alone in a secluded location, he had no idea how he was going to do it.

"Is everyone in place?" he asked.

"Yep," Danielle said. "Ms. Skoglund is outside, and we just got a report that Lobo is on his way."

"And you tested everything, right?"

"More than once."

As he waited, his fingers absently rubbed the medallion that Grandpa had given him. One minute he was worried that Lobo was going to walk through the door and shoot him; the next minute he was concerned that Lobo wasn't going to show up at all.

There was no knock. The door simply opened, its rusted hinges resisting as Ms. Skoglund walked in. Her cheeks and nose were bright red, and she looked out of breath. "This place looks a lot different at night," she said as her eyes fell on a sickle that hung in the storage room. "It's definitely creepier."

The door shut with a click, and Colt watched as she stood there as though listening for something in particular. She cocked her head and frowned, but then she shrugged. "So," she said, sounding strangely casual given the circumstances, "do I look conspiratorial enough?" She held her arms out and spun in a slow circle; she was dressed in black from her stocking cap to her boots.

"More like a cat burglar, but yeah, I guess so," Colt said.

She walked over to one of the windows and peered out across the lawn. "Are you nervous?"

"A little."

"Me too," she said, turning to him and smiling. "The anticipation is the hard part. Once he walks through that door, you're going to be great."

"Okay," Danielle said. "He's pulling up now, and he's not alone."

"Is it Krone?" Colt asked.

"We think so, but we aren't sure."

The sound of tires crunching over gravel broke the silence, and Colt ran over to join Ms. Skoglund at the window. They watched Lobo pull up in his silver Mercedes G550 SUV and cut the lights before he shut down the engine. He stepped out of the vehicle and onto the drive, but Krone wasn't sitting in the passenger seat. It was Agent Graves, which meant Krone was out there somewhere, unaccounted for.

"Now what?" Colt asked.

"We improvise," Ms. Skoglund said.

They walked back over to the center aisle and tried to act inconspicuous. Colt could feel his heart beating in his throat and his palms itched.

Then the door swung open.

:: CHAPTER 45 ::

Director Romero? What are you doing here?" Ms. Skoglund asked, her eyes wide with shock.

"I'm sorry," Lobo said, smiling as he walked into the light. "I didn't mean to interrupt." Instead of a uniform, he was dressed casually in a ski jacket, blue jeans, and work boots. Agent Graves stood behind him in a driving cap, scarf, and a long coat that was big enough to hide at least one gun.

"You didn't. It's just that . . . well . . ." Ms. Skoglund looked at the floorboards. "I know this might seem strange, but . . ."

"Now that you mention it, a midnight rendezvous between a teacher and student is a bit odd," Lobo said, his manner calm. "Particularly since Cadet McAlister isn't in any of your classes. Or am I mistaken?"

"No, sir, you're not."

"It's not her fault," Colt said. "I asked her to meet me."

Lobo raised a single eyebrow.

"I overheard my grandpa on the phone this afternoon," Colt said. "He was talking about something called Operation Nemesis, but when I asked him about it, he wouldn't tell me anything. I figured Ms. Skoglund would know what it was."

"And what did you find out?"

Colt looked over at Ms. Skoglund, then stared at the ground.

"That's not an answer," Lobo said. He took a step toward Colt and his eyes narrowed. "Tell me what you know."

"That it had something to do with Senator Bishop . . . and that he didn't die from a heart attack." Colt made sure he was looking directly into Lobo's eyes. "He was murdered."

"I haven't seen mention of that in any of the reports."

Colt shrugged. "Your name came up too."

"Really?"

"They think you did it."

Lobo grabbed him by the shirt and drove him against a post. "Don't play games with me, boy," he said, his lip curled into a snarl. "I want to know everything that you heard."

Colt struggled to breathe, and Lobo relaxed his grip, though not by much. "Operation Nemesis is a covert project where you're working with an assassin to eliminate people like Senator Bishop, or anyone else who threatens to cut your funding or replace you."

"I don't suppose you were accessing files that you weren't supposed to see, were you, Kirsten?" Lobo asked, though he didn't bother looking at Ms. Skoglund.

"It doesn't matter," Colt said. "They already knew."

"And who is *they*?"

"The Department of Alien Affairs. They've been investigating you for over a year."

Lobo smiled. "They need me, you know. The politicians might not admit it—not to you or the reporters or the sheep that vote them into office, but it's true. They rely on men like me to do the work they aren't willing to do."

"Murdering innocent people?"

"Innocent? Tell me something . . . when the Thule come in force—and they will—who do you think will stand on the front lines? The politicians? Their sons and daughters? Of course not. Yet they sit in their ivory towers and slash our funding so they can pander to voters . . . the same voters who will be slaughtered because we don't have the weapons to defend ourselves. And I'm the murderer? I've done everything I can to save the masses, and if that calls for a few casualties along the way, then so be it!"

As Colt watched over Lobo's shoulder, Agent Graves morphed into Heinrich Krone. The assassin pulled out an H&K USP 45 with a tactical light mounted beneath the barrel. He pointed it at Ms. Skoglund, and that's when the lights went out.

She took advantage of the diversion and ducked behind the old Ford before he could fire his weapon. At the same time, a red light no bigger than the tip of a drinking straw danced across Krone's chest. It bobbed like a gnat until it landed in the middle of his forehead.

"Get down!" Lobo shouted.

There was a pop, followed by the sound of shattering glass. A tranquilizer dart ripped through the barn, narrowly missing Krone before it bit into the wall. At the same time, metal canisters the size of soda cans broke through the windows, filling the room with noxious smoke.

Men in riot gear burst through doors and windows, the beams from their tactical lights crisscrossing through the darkness like incandescent threads of spiderweb. They were dressed in black from their helmets and ski masks to their gloves and boots. Each wore infrared goggles, and they were armed. Colt thought he could see Giru Ba, and he couldn't tell if Grandpa was standing next to the Ford. His eyes burned from all the smoke.

"We'll take the tunnels!" Lobo ran toward one of the stalls, but Krone hesitated. He dug into his pocket, pulled out a concussion grenade, and set the detonator.

"Grenade!" Colt shouted.

The safe choice would have been to get as far away from the barn as he could, but when Colt heard the sound of a door slamming shut, he knew where Lobo and Krone had gone. There must have been an entrance to the underground tunnel system hidden in the floorboards, and Colt wasn't about to let them get away. He dived into the stall and scrambled on his hands and knees, his fingers searching for the entrance.

"Come on!"

His fingers finally found a brass handle on the floor, and he pried the trapdoor open as a shockwave shook the building. Bats shrieked, windows exploded, and the ceiling caved in as he slipped into the darkness. He didn't fall far, but the ground was hard and air burst out of his lungs.

The darkness was suffocating, and the walls felt like a tomb as he lay still, listening for any sound of Lobo or Krone. All he could hear was a constant ringing sound, which he figured was an aftereffect of the grenade. He pulled out his LED flashlight and flicked it on. He was in an empty room with cement block walls and a low ceiling that exposed rafters overrun by cobwebs.

"Colt . . . can you hear me?" Danielle asked. Her voice sounded faint, and there was a slight crackle, but Colt was just happy that he wasn't deaf. "Please tell me you made it out of there."

"Not exactly." He stood on uneasy legs. "I'm in some kind of cellar under the barn. Where's Ms. Skoglund?"

"She's safe, and so is your grandpa," Danielle said. "Did you see what happened to Lobo and Krone?"

"They're down here with me."

"What?"

Colt walked over to a wooden door that creaked as he opened it. On the other side was a narrow corridor choked in shadow. "It looks like the cellar connects with that tunnel system beneath the campus. There's no way we're going to find him."

"Wait a minute," Danielle said.

Colt could hear what sounded like a zipper, followed by a sound of shuffling papers. "Okay, I found the map that shows the tunnel system. I can't see any other entry or exit points near the barn."

"What about the river?" If Lobo couldn't get to his SUV, the water was his best bet for escape.

"There's a boathouse about a quarter mile north."

"That's where he went."

"But—"

"Look, I know what you're going to say, but I have to finish this," Colt said. "Tell Giru Ba to send a team of agents over there, and I'll make sure they don't come back this way."

"You're going to get yourself killed."

"I'll be okay. But I'm going to need your help."

He decided not to use the flashlight. Lobo and Krone would be able to see a light long before he saw either of them. He'd rely on Danielle and her map to guide him through the twists and turns instead.

"Okay, you should see a slow curve up to the left," Danielle said. "Once you make it past that, it should only be about two hundred yards to the boathouse."

Colt stopped. He thought he heard voices. He crept forward, careful not to shuffle or scrape his boot against the ground. Up ahead, tiny eyes flashed yellow, and he could just make out the silhouette of what looked like a possum or a very large rat. It stared at him for a long moment before it turned and skittered into the shadows.

Suddenly the silence was overwhelming. The voices had stopped, but Colt pressed forward, each step an act of the will. His mouth was dry. His hands itched. He turned cautiously around the corner and something heavy hit him in the chest, knocking him to the ground.

:: CHAPTER 46 ::

I don't know whether to be impressed or annoyed," Lobo said as he kicked Colt in the ribs. Pain shot through Colt's body as he writhed on the ground, wondering if that was what it felt like to get hit by a locomotive.

"Krone set you up," Colt said through clenched teeth. The words spilled from his tongue before he knew what he was saying, but judging from the expression on Lobo's face, it struck a nerve.

"What are you talking about?"

"I'm not the target, you are."

Krone walked over and leveled his gun at Colt. "Those DAA agents will be here any minute," he said to Lobo, as the beam from the tactical light burned in Colt's eyes.

"Do you know how many chances he's had to kill me?" Colt said, his eyes fixed on Lobo as he tried to stall. "I saw him standing outside our window back home. He had a clean shot, but he didn't take it. Or what about the rodeo? Or even the car chase? How did Ms. Skoglund run him off the road? It's not like she's a professional driver or anything. She's the only CHAOS agent who isn't allowed to carry a gun."

"That's enough!" Krone's nostrils flared.

"He wants to get rid of you because he knows that you're the only thing that stands between us and them," Colt said, desperate to appeal to Lobo's ego.

Krone lashed out, striking Colt in the face with the butt of his gun. It opened a gash beneath his eye, and blood poured down his cheek.

"It's true!" Colt ignored the pain as he pulled the Bola Cuffs out of his pocket and flicked them at Krone. Weighted ropes shot out as the disc struck the assassin in the chest. They wrapped around his shoulders and pinned his arms to his side, and Krone fell, flailing on the ground as his gun bounced into the shadows.

"That's an impressive trick, but I'm afraid it won't save you." Lobo reached into his jacket and pulled out a Sig Sauer P226 with a silencer.

"I never asked for any of this," Colt said. He held his arms out wide, trying to show that he wasn't a threat. "I don't want to run CHAOS . . . I don't even want to go to this school. If I had my choice, I'd be back in San Diego with my parents, but that's not exactly an option."

Lobo raised the weapon, his hand steady and his face devoid of emotion. "Once you're gone, they'll realize that they should never have placed their hope in some ridiculous prophecy," he said. "I am the only one who can save us from the coming onslaught."

There was an echo of footsteps as someone came running down the tunnel.

"Dad, no!" Oz was out of breath, and his face was twisted in confusion—like he was trying to get his mind to accept what his eyes already knew. His father was a murderer.

"You shouldn't be here," Lobo said.

"Why? Are you afraid that I'll see who you really are?"

Lobo smiled, but the expression held only sorrow. "I didn't have a choice. They were going to take everything away from me . . . from us . . ."

Krone bellowed as he continued to fight against the bindings that held him. His bones cracked and his skin turned to scales as two extra sets of arms grew out of his back. The man was gone, replaced by one of the Thule. It flexed once, and the Bola Cuffs snapped like they were made of twine.

Blinded by its rage, Krone attacked indiscriminately. The monster charged at Lobo, who fired three shots into its chest, but it wasn't even fazed. Krone grabbed him by the face and threw him against the wall. Then it spun and its tail battered Oz, sending him to the ground.

The monster charged at Colt with jaws wide, but he rolled out of the way before it could bite him in half. Incensed, Krone grabbed him by the shoulders and lifted him off the ground. Colt kicked to break free, and as he did, he could see Oz inching toward his dad's gun. He stood up on shaky legs and leveled the barrel at the Thule.

"Wait!" Colt shouted, afraid that he might get hit by a stray bullet.

"Relax," Oz said. "It's just like target practice back in the desert . . . Aim. Exhale. And then pull the trigger." He unloaded four shots, burying the bullets in the monster's back. The sound of its scream echoed through the tunnels as dirt and rock fell from the ceiling. Krone dropped Colt as Oz fired three more times, but the monster wouldn't fall.

Oz fired three more shots as the monster ran toward him with arms extended. Then two more. The magazine was empty, but Krone didn't stop. It swung, and as Oz ducked, its claws ripped through the wall.

"Hey, ugly!"

Krone turned to find Colt holding two silver canisters like he was a gunslinger in the Wild West. He sprayed the foam on the monster's feet and watched it expand. Krone tried to lift its legs, but they were cemented in place. Enraged, it beat its tail against the wall, and one of the rafters cracked.

"Come on," Colt said. "We have to get out of here before there's a cave-in."

"What about my dad?" Oz asked.

"Do you think you can carry him?"

"I can try." Oz went to where Lobo lay, unconscious. The dirt around his head was saturated with blood, and his breathing was shallow.

"Hurry up," Colt said, looking at the Thule. "I don't think that stuff is going to hold."

No sooner had the words left his mouth than the foam started to crack.

"Get him out of here!" Colt said. "I'll take care of Krone."

"Are you sure?"

"Go!"

Oz threw his dad over his shoulder and headed back down the tunnel, leaving Colt alone with the monster. It ran at him, but Colt dodged and struck it in the ribs with a palm strike. It swung again, but missed, smashing the wall.

There was no way he should have been able to dodge all six arms, but he did, weaving in and out, ducking and falling back. The Thule pressed the attack, but the monster couldn't touch him.

It was as though Colt had some kind of extrasensory perception. Then he realized what was happening. It wasn't him . . . it was the alien DNA. It was both terrifying and exhilarating, but he didn't have time to dwell on it.

Colt slammed his fist into the monster's jaw, and its head snapped back. He followed it with an upper cut and then a palm strike to the snout. The monster wailed as Colt swung again, but that time it caught him by the wrist.

For a brief moment Colt's feet dangled in the air before the monster threw him across the corridor. Pain erupted as Colt slammed into brick. He tried to stand, but Krone grabbed him by the back of his neck and threw him once more.

As he lay there Colt could feel Grandpa's medallion as it hung around his neck. The verse on the back promised that God would be his refuge and his strength in times of trouble, and if he ever needed strength, it was now. He could hear the monster's heavy breathing as rough hands picked him up and drove him into the wall.

"Help me . . ."

Timbers cracked overhead, threatening to break as more debris fell. The rafters wouldn't hold the ceiling back for much longer. Before Colt could catch his breath, the monster wrapped a clawed hand around his face. It felt like a vise, and no matter how hard he tried, Colt couldn't break free. Then an idea popped into his head. He pulled out the flashlight and shined the beam in Krone's eyes.

Temporarily blinded, the Thule dropped him. Its tail pounded against the wall and the tunnel shook, sending chunks of earth falling from the ceiling. Colt drove his shoulder into the monster's stomach, but it pounded him in the back, sending Colt to the ground. Then it tried to crush him with its foot, but Colt rolled out of the way.

"You are not the Betrayer!" it bellowed. "We are coming! And when we do, we will destroy your world!" The monster lashed out with opened claws, looking to rip through Colt's skin and into his vital organs.

"Not on my watch!" Colt ducked out of the way and struck Krone in the abdomen with double fists. The monster followed up with a hammer strike, but Colt rolled between its legs and connected with a heel kick to the back of its knee, followed by an elbow to the base of its neck.

Krone howled and swung a massive arm that caught Colt in the chest, knocking him against the wall. The monster tried to bite him, but Colt recovered and kicked it in the snout. Then, with a running leap, he used the wall as a springboard and landed on its shoulders. He wrapped his legs around the monster's throat and squeezed as he hit Krone repeatedly in the head. Krone snapped its jaws as it reached for Colt. One hand caught him in the shoulder, and sharp claws tore through his jacket and the ballistic vest. Another hand grabbed him around the arm and ripped him away.

Colt flipped through the air before landing on his shoulder and skidding across the ground until he smashed into the wall. His body ached, but he was determined to end it. He ran at Krone, using the monster's arms like monkey bars until he was standing on its shoulders. He didn't hesitate as he grabbed hold of a splintered rafter and pulled. The beam snapped, and Colt dropped to the ground before running to get clear of the cave-in.

There was a rumble, and the tunnel started to shake. Confused, the monster watched as the broken rafter struck it in the shoulder.

A moment later the ceiling fell, and Krone was buried under a massive pile of dirt and rock.

As Colt stood in the darkness, he knew that Grandpa was right. There was no glory in killing someone—even when you didn't have a choice.

:: CHAPTER 47 ::

Santiago Romero's arrest was the lead story for just about every news agency across the globe. He had been linked to the murders of two United States senators, the deputy director of the CIA's National Clandestine Service, a federal judge, and Agent Graves, who had found out about Operation Nemesis and threatened to expose Lobo if he didn't turn himself in.

There was speculation that CHAOS was going to shut down, but during a joint press conference with the Department of Alien Affairs it was announced that Ezekiel Watson, the director of the DAA, would assume control of CHAOS, and deputy director Abigail Thorne would run the day-to-day operations—including the CHAOS Military Academy.

Classes were cancelled the following week to give the new leadership time to transition. That gave Colt plenty of time to answer questions down at DAA headquarters, where investigators asked about everything from his involvement with the Romero family to whether or not he believed that aliens should expect the same constitutional freedoms that were shared by humans. It was monotonous, and at times annoying, but at least he didn't have to look over his shoulder worrying that someone was going to shoot at him or stab him with a syringe.

By the time Friday afternoon rolled around, he was exhausted. All he wanted to do was grab something to eat and go to bed, but Danielle tracked him down and said she needed his help with a project. He should have known something was up when she wouldn't tell him what it was.

They met at seven o'clock on the front steps of the library. Danielle was holding a box, and inside was a triple layer chocolate cake with chocolate butter cream frosting. She had baked it from scratch with a little help from Ms. Skoglund.

"I don't get it," Colt said. "This is your project?"

"It's Oz's birthday," she said. "I thought we could surprise him."

Colt felt his stomach churn. He hadn't talked to Oz in almost a week, in part because he didn't know what to say. Just that morning prosecutors announced that they would seek the death penalty for Lobo.

"Maybe you should go without me," Colt said.

"You're going to have to talk to him sooner or later. Besides, he really needs you right now."

"Yeah, right." Colt found the thought almost laughable. "I'm the one who tricked his dad into a confession and basically ruined his life. I'm probably the last person he wants to see."

"You might be surprised."

Colt followed her up the steps and into a foyer where everything was made of stone, from the floor to the pillars to the sweeping arches. She went up another flight of stairs and down a long corridor until she stopped at a simple wooden door with a brass knob.

"Wait until you see this."

She opened the door into a storage room. Cardboard boxes, books, and supplies like lightbulbs and printer paper filled the metal shelves, but that's not why Danielle had brought him there. Resting against the far wall were five enormous posters featuring covers from the *Phantom Flyer and the Agents of CHAOS* comic book series, including the issue that had the first appearance of Intellitron.

Next to those was a mannequin dressed in vintage flight pants, boots, and a leather bomber jacket. Its face was covered by a gas mask and aviator goggles, and it was wearing a helmet and a jet pack.

"Recognize anything?" Danielle was smiling as she watched Colt from the corner of her eye.

"Is that my Grandpa's stuff?"

"He loaned everything to them for the Phantom Flyer exhibition next month," she said. "I thought that since Oz was such a big fan, this would be the perfect place to celebrate his birthday. I mean, I know it's basically a closet, but the curator said it would be okay. What do you think?"

"It's incredible."

"I'm glad you like it. Now help me set up the table before he gets here."

Colt unfolded the legs of a card table while Danielle took a white tablecloth out of her backpack. She set out plates and forks, and she even had a Phantom Flyer action figure for a cake topper.

There was a knock at the door, then it opened and Oz stuck his head in. "Danielle? You in here?" He looked tired. His eyes were heavy and his shoulders slumped.

"Happy birthday!" Danielle shouted as she ran over and gave him a hug.

"Yeah," Colt said. "Happy birthday."

Oz smiled when he saw the cake, but when he opened the small package Danielle handed him, he really lit up. Inside was a vintage Phantom Flyer signet ring that looked just like the one Colt's dad had saved cereal box tops to get when he was a kid.

"Do you know how hard these are to find? Where did you get it?" Oz asked as he slipped it on his finger.

Danielle shrugged. "Does it matter?"

"It's just that they're really expensive."

"If you don't think you're worth it, I can always take it back," she said, holding out her hand.

"Sorry," he said. "But this ring is never leaving my finger."

They ate cake and reminisced about home, wondering about their friends. Colt thought about Lily, and how every guy in the school had probably asked her out by now. He wondered if she had a boyfriend, or if she was too busy writing music.

Eventually the conversation turned to their new lives at the CHAOS Military Academy, and how quickly everything had changed.

"How's your dad?" Danielle asked as Oz scooped up some frosting with his finger.

"He left the hospital yesterday, and it looks like they're going to transfer him to Leavenworth until the trial is over. But that could take years."

Danielle reached over and grabbed his hand. "I'm so sorry about what happened. I can't imagine what you're going through."

"Thanks."

"I'm sorry too," Colt said. "I mean, we should have told you about Operation Nemesis as soon we found out. It's just that . . . I don't know. I guess I was scared, but that doesn't make it right."

"I would have done the same thing," Oz said. "Besides, after everything that's happened, I'm the one who should apologize. I still can't believe my dad was a part of all that. It makes me sick."

"Just remember, you aren't your dad," Colt said.

"I guess."

"So what happens now?" Danielle asked. "Are you still thinking about transferring?"

"I talked to Agent Thorne," Oz said. "I told her that I want to stay."

Danielle's eyes lit up. "Seriously?"

"If Colt is going to lead us against the Thule, somebody is going to have to watch his back. What kind of friend would I be if I bailed on him now?" He held out his hand. "Brothers to the end, right?"

Colt grasped it. "Brothers to the end."

|||||||||||||||||||||||||||||||||||||

Grandpa was at the kitchen table reading his Bible when Colt walked through the front door of the small apartment. He had helped himself to another thick slice of Danielle's decadent cake, but he was still hungry, so he walked over to the freezer and pulled out a carton of butter pecan ice cream. "Do you want some?" he asked as he searched through the drawers for a scoop.

"Maybe later," Grandpa said. "How did everything go tonight?"

"Okay, I guess. Danielle's big project was actually a surprise birthday party for Oz."

"You don't say."

"We had cake over at the library," Colt said. "She decorated the room in a Phantom Flyer theme. Why didn't you tell me about the exhibition? After all, it's in your honor."

"I guess it slipped my mind." He placed a red satin bookmark between the pages and closed his Bible. "Look, I know things have been a bit crazy lately."

"A bit?"

"Unfortunately, it may get a whole lot crazier."

Colt took another bite of his ice cream. "Is that even possible?"

"A Thule warship crashed near Groom Lake in Nevada around four this morning. There was only one survivor, and he's in a coma."

Colt put down his spoon. "Where did it come from?"

"By all indications the Thule were able to create a gateway, but it was only open long enough to let the one ship through." Grandpa rubbed the bridge of his nose with his thumb and forefinger. "I used to think we had decades to prepare before they would find a way to bring their hordes. At this rate, they'll be here by Christmas."

CLASSIFIED

TOP SECRET

Colt McAllister fought the Thule and
lived to tell about it.

But now he`s been captured and taken
to their planet—and if he can`t find a
way to escape, Earth will be gone.

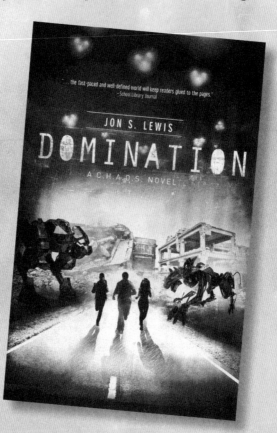

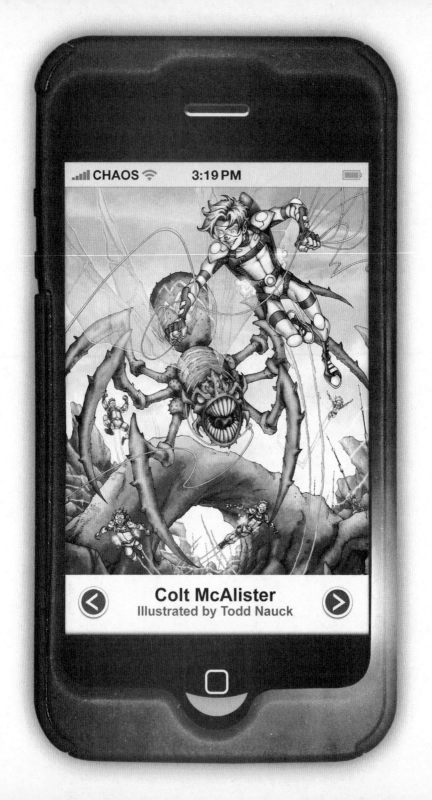

Colt McAlister

Illustrated by Todd Nauck

Oz Romero
Illustrated by Enrique Rivera

Danielle Salazar
Illustrated by Danny Araya

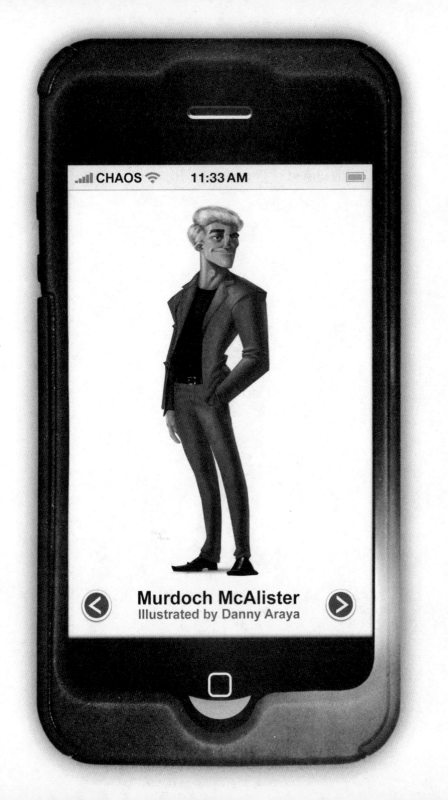

Murdoch McAlister
Illustrated by Danny Araya

Major General Walker
Illustrated by Danny Araya

CHAOS 1:18 AM

Lobo Romero
Illustrated by Enrique Rivera

Thule
Illustrated by Danny Araya

Creating Comics

By Jon S. Lewis

I t's exciting to see how popular graphic novels have become. I grew up on comic books. The moment my parents plopped that allowance money into my hand, I'd hop on my bike and head over to the dime store where there was a spinner rack stuffed with *Action Comics, Fantastic Four, The Amazing Spider-Man, Justice League of America*, and tons more. I was able to buy five comics each week, and I'd stand there for hours thumbing through each title and wondering how I was going to narrow my choices. It wasn't easy. Eventually I'd make it home where I'd run to my bedroom, shut the door, grab a stack of paper, a pencil, and black pen, and then I'd start drawing my favorite panels. More often than not, it featured Benjamin Jacob Grimm, a.k.a. The Thing (who was also on my lunchbox).

My purchasing habits haven't changed much, but instead of riding my bike to the nearest dime store, I drive to Greg's Comics. I still spend hours poring over the amazing art, and I've learned to appreciate the storytelling of not just the words but the images as well.

I've been lucky enough to write for DC Comics, which has

been a childhood dream come true. My editor, Shannon Eric Denton, helped me understand the difference between writing a novel and writing a comic book. In traditional prose, writers have a lot of real estate to work with. Most novels end up in the 65,000-90,000 word range, which is usually somewhere between 250-400 pages. In a comic book, there are only 22 pages.

Writing a comic book must be easier, right? I mean, after all, it's way shorter. But there's a catch. You have to tell an entire story in those 22 pages—the same story that you'd tell in an entire novel. Oh, and you can't write any descriptive text. All you get is dialogue. Still think it's easier?

Writing comic books is a fantastic exercise for writing traditional prose, because it teachers you the economy of words. In today's headline society, few of us read the newspaper from front-to-back (let alone a physical newspaper). We're so busy that we only have time to read the headlines. That's why novels need to grab our attention right away—and they can't slow down. Once a reader gets bored, he's not going to come back and finish it.

Books need to be tight. That means cutting the fluff. Writing comic books teaches you how to write an exciting, complete story with an extremely limited word count. It also forces you to make sure your dialogue is strong. A great way to test dialogue is to read it out loud. Or you could even give the pages to a couple of friends and listen to them read it out loud. If the dialogue sounds goofy or unnatural, it probably is. Then you can go back in and tweak it until it sounds like something someone would actually say.

My favorite component of writing comic books and graphic novels is that it's truly a collaborative process. You work with not just an editor, but with a team of artists: a penciller, inker, colorist, and a letterer. Writing a novel is solitary—like living alone in a cave on top of a remote mountain peak. With comic books, you have an entire team to bounce ideas back and forth, and it's energizing!

You end up working closest with the penciller. He's the one who turns your words into images. Some people operate in what's been coined "The Marvel Method." It started in the early days at Marvel Comics, where Stan Lee would come up with a story idea, hand it off to an artist, and that artist would flesh into 22 pages of amazing illustrations. When he was done, Stan would go back and fill in the word balloons with dialogue and voila!

I prefer a more traditional method. I write the story and break it into panels (the squares and rectangles that frame all the illustrations on each page). I break out the dialogue and write notes about what I envisioned for the illustrations. It's a lot like a director on a movie set. I talk about things like camera angles (close up, wideshot, aerial view, etc.), and then I explain backgrounds and which characters should be in each panel. But that's not always what makes it to the final page.

Comic book artists are some of the best illustrators and storytellers in the world, and sometimes they have a vision for the art that's different from mine. And you know what? I love it! I'm a firm believer that differing views not only make this world interesting, but they bring about greatness. I love to be challenged, because it forces me to consider that there might be a better way of doing something. That's true collaboration, and when someone challenges you in life it shows they have passion.

Once the penciller and I have agreed on the panel layouts, he starts to draw. When his drawings are approved, the inker goes over the pencils to finalize those bold lines and powerful shadows. Then it's up to the colorist to make it all pop. When he's done, the letterer goes in and creates the word balloons.

For the prologue to *Alienation*, I was lucky enough to work with Mike Dubisch. He not only did the pencils, but he inked and lettered the pages as well. That's real talent!

For those of you who want to become writers, comic books and graphic novels are an exciting format. In fact, we've included the manuscript that Mike and I worked from. Now you have an insider's edge to creating your own stories.

See next pages for how the Graphic Novel Prologue was written.

WRITING COMICS

DIRECTIONS FOR GRAPHIC NOVEL PROLOGUE

PAGE ONE (refer to page ix at front)

Panel 1

EXPLORATION TEAM WALKING THROUGH GRECIAN RUINS, LED BY AN OLDER BRITISH MAN WITH A HANDLEBAR MUSTACHE (LORD FRANCIS BEEDLES). BESIDES BEEDLES, THERE SHOULD BE AT LEAST ONE WOMAN, AND A MALE FROM INDIA WHO IS CARRYING AN ENORMOUS PACK AND POSSIBLY A BLUNDERBUSS (FASHION CIRCA 1907). IT DOESN'T NEED TO BE A LARGE GROUP (MAYBE FIVE PEOPLE IN ALL).

Caption (1): In 1907, Lord Francis Beedles led a team of explorers to the Greek island of Crete. They were looking for the labyrinth where Theseus slew the Minotaur. What they discovered was even more remarkable.

Panel 2

BEEDLES HOLDS UP A TORCH TO REVEAL STRANGE PICTOGRAPHS OF THE THULE (WALKING LIZARDS WITH SIX ARMS, TWO LEGS AND A TAIL–REFERENCE AVAILABLE). FACES SHOULD REVEAL SHOCK AND CONFUSION.

Caption (2): Deep inside a cave near the ruins of Knossos were pictographs of strange creatures that looked like walking lizards. It was a curious find.

Panel 3

THE GATEWAY SHOULD BE SOME KIND OF DOORWAY INSIDE THE TUNNEL SYSTEM OF THE CAVES. IT COULD BE RINGED WITH GLYPHS, ARCHED OR SQUARED. REGARDLESS, WE NEED A SENSE THAT IT IS MORE THAN AN OPENING . . . IT IS A GATEWAY TO ANOTHER WORLD. MAYBE THERE'S SOME KIND OF GLOW, OR SOMEONE REACHING A HAND THROUGH AND IT'S SWALLOWED BY THE DARKNESS SO YOU CAN NO LONGER SEE IT.

Caption (3): So was the gateway, a door that somehow led them to a strange new world . . .

Panel 4
BEEDLES IS HIDDEN AS HE DISCOVERS A SCENE WITH AT LEAST ONE
OF THE THULE STANDING THERE, AND POSSIBLY MORE.

Caption (4): A world populated by the very creatures they had
found on the walls.

PAGE TWO

Panel 1
JEREMIAH HIBBIT (ABOUT 28-35 YEARS OLD) IS RUNNING WITH ONE
OF THE THULE CHASING AFTER HIM. IT WOULD BE NICE TO SHOW
HIS CAMERA . . . SOMETHING HE IS HOLDING ON TO AS A PRIZED
POSSESSION.

Caption (1): Of the seven explorers, only one returned—a pho-
tographer by the name of Jeremiah Hibbit.

Panel 2
PHOTOS OF STRANGE CREATURES SPREAD HAPHAZARDLY ACROSS A
TABLE.

Caption (2): He brought back pictures, but they were dismissed as
fakes.

Panel 3
SHOW ONE OF THE THULE IN EITHER LONDON OR TOKYO (CIRCA
1900-1915).

Caption (3): Soon bizarre creatures were spotted in places like
London, Tokyo, and New York City. For the gateway worked both
ways.

Panel 4
SHOW A MAN SKULKING ABOUT IN THE SEWERS (CIRCA 1900-1915).
HE'S BEEN SPOTTED BY SOMEONE WEARING A HARDHAT WITH A
LIGHT (SOME KIND OF SANITATION WORKER). LOTS OF SHADOWS
AND PERHAPS THE PERSON DISCOVERED HAS GLOWING EYES.

Caption (4): Some witnesses even claimed that the creatures could shapeshift.

Panel 5
THE MAN HAS TURNED INTO A HULKING THULE.

No dialogue or caption.

PAGE THREE

Panel 1
SHOW SOLDIERS AS THOUGH THEY ARE POSING FOR A PHOTOGRAPH. THE CENTER FIGURE IS THE PHANTOM FLYER (REFERENCE AVAILABLE).

Caption (1): Years later there were rumors that Hitler found an enclave of the lizard men, and that he enlisted to fight in his army.

Panel 2
BATTLE SCENE WITH AT LEAST ONE THULE FIGHTING ONE OR TWO US SOLDIERS. THE THULE SHOULD TOWER OVER THEM (ABOUT 7-8 FEET TALL VS. 6 FEET TALL).

Caption (2): In response, the United States formed the Central Headquarters Against the Occult and Supernatural.

Panel 3
SHOW THE THULE OVERWHELMING ANOTHER ALIEN RACE.

Caption (3): CHAOS agents learned that the lizard men were a race of warmongers known as the Thule.

Panel 4
SHOW THE THULE FIGHTING BESIDE NAZIS (AND A NAZI ROBOT).

Caption (4): Over the centuries they had expanded their empire by destroying world after world. Now that their own planet was dying, they sought the Earth as their new home.

PAGE FOUR

Panel 1
SOMETHING TO SHOW THAT THE ALIENS ARE HIDING AMONG US.

Caption (1): After the Allies defeated Hitler, the Thule went into hiding. They waited as their scientists invented a technology that could open a gateway large enough for their machines of war.

Panel 2
SHOW AN AERIAL VIEW OF THE EARTH AS THOUGH IT IS BEING TAKEN FROM OUTERSPACE. POSSIBLY SHOW A SPACESHIP OR AN ARMADA.

Caption (2): The Earth would be theirs, for according to an ancient prophecy, they would never know defeat . . .

Panel 3
SHOW "THE BETRAYER" (A THULE) STANDING WITH HIS ARMS IN THE AIR AND HIS HEAD THROWN BACK, WITH THULE LYING AT HIS FEET, UNCONSCIOUS.

Caption (3): That is until one of their own blood—The Betrayer—would turn against his people. On that day, their Empire will crumble.

PAGE FIVE

Panel 1
SHOW AN ALIEN POW BEING PARADED IN FRONT OF US SOLDIERS.

Caption (1): When American troops learned about the prophecy, it gave them an idea . . .

Panel 2
SHOW A GI INJECTING HIMSELF WITH BLOOD. SHOW AN ALIEN CADAVER NEARBY . . . BUT HAVE IT BE WHOLE WITH ITS ARMS ACROSS ITS CHEST (NO GORE).

Caption (2): Desperate to end the war, GIs injected themselves with the blood from an alien cadaver. They hoped it would turn at least one of them into the Betrayer.

Panel 3

SHOW A DOCTOR INJECTING A CHILD WITH A SYRINGE AND NEEDLE. MAYBE THE CAMERA IS IN THE CEILING LOOKING DOWN AT A CHILD WHO IS LYING ON AN OPERATING TABLE LOOKING SCARED AS THE DOCTOR IS ABOUT TO INJECT HIM.

Caption (3): It didn't work. But the United States government adapted the test and secretly injected thousands of men and boys with a serum that contained alien DNA.

Panel 4

SHOW COLT MCALISTER (THE 16-YEAR-OLD STAR OF THE BOOK SERIES) FLYING THROUGH THE SKY IN A JET PACK, COMING TOWARD THE CAMERA. HE'S DRESSED IN A 1940S BOMBER JACKET AND IS WEARING AVIATOR GOGGLES AND A JET PACK. HE HAS LONG, BLOND HAIR FLOWING IN THE WIND.

Caption (4): It took more than fifty years, but they finally found a match.

Caption (5): As the Thule prepare to invade, our leaders pray that Colt McAlister truly is the one . . . that he is the Betrayer.

- END -

BIG QUESTIONS

1. One of the stipulations for attending the CHAOS Military Academy is that cadets are not allowed to use cell phones, portable music players, or laptop computers. They have no access to the Internet or their families for eighteen months. What would it take for you to make that kind of sacrifice?

2. The night before Colt moved to Virginia, agents from the Department of Alien Affairs detained him. They detained Lily too. Colt wanted to call her and apologize for what happened, but he was worried that she'd be upset, so he put it off until it was too late. Are you the kind of person who prefers to ignore interpersonal conflict, hoping that time will help the problem disappear? Or do you like to talk things out right away and get it over with?

3. Colt has strong romantic feelings toward Lily. In fact, he thinks that he might be in love, but he isn't sure. What are the odds of two sixteen-year-olds falling in love and staying together for the rest of their lives? Do you know married couples that met when they were in high school?

4. Colt went through a series of dangerous tests sanctioned by the United States government when he was a child. They wiped his memory, but his parents and his grandfather knew about them. They never told him. When Colt finally found out they knew, he felt betrayed. Is withholding the truth the same as lying? Is there ever a time when withholding the truth or lying would be the upright thing to do?

5. All his life Colt dreamed of saving the world from supervillains and alien invasions. But now that he has the chance to actually do it, he isn't sure if he's ready. Has there been a time in your life when you were called on to do something, but you didn't feel qualified? What happened?

6. Colt appreciates that Danielle tells him the truth, even when it might upset him. Do you have friends in your life who are willing to be honest with you, even if it means that you might get upset? Are you willing to be honest with your friends regardless of their reactions?

7. Pierce Bowen attacks a cadet at the CHAOS Military Academy because he was different. Colt steps in to protect the cadet even though he risks getting jumped by Pierce and his friends. What would you do if you saw someone getting bullied?

8. In the book, government agents manipulate evidence and two career criminals are incarcerated for crimes they didn't commit. Do you think governments have that kind of power? If so, do you think they're willing to exercise that power?

9. In the story, Colt's grandfather talks about seeing fellow soldiers die in combat. He thinks video games glorify death. Do you agree? Is there anything wrong with killing people in a video game?

10. Colt's grandfather gives him a medallion inscribed with Psalm 46:1. It states that *God is our refuge and strength, a very present help in trouble.* Has there been a time in your life where that was true?

TEAM THANKS

I don't remember a time when I didn't love comic books. Maybe it started with the Spider-Man segment on *Electric Company*. Or it could have been the Super Friends Saturday morning cartoon. There was the Marvel superheroes lunchbox that I had in kindergarten (the one where my mom always packed Spaghettios in my thermos), and reruns of the live-action *Batman* series starring Adam West. Regardless of where it all started, I wish novels took a page from comic books. You see, the title page on a comic book doesn't just list the writer, but it also lists the artists, editors, and sometimes the executives who work tirelessly behind the scenes.

This book wouldn't have happened without contributions that went way above the norm, starting with Lee Hough from Alive Communications. He is not only the best agent in the business, but he's a wonderful mentor and sounding board. As I write this, Lee is battling a Boogeyman in the form of a cancerous brain tumor. So if you're the praying sort, remember Lee and his family as he gets ready for radiation and chemo.

I am honored to work with Thomas Nelson's incredible team, and in particular, Amanda Bostic and Allen Arnold. They were encouraging, patient, and are a talented and innovative team with an astounding vision. I'd also like to thank Becky Monds, Eric Mullett, Ashley Schneider, and Kristen Vasgaard.

Thank you to LB Norton for jumping into the eye of a hurricane and offering a sense of calm and finesse. She worked around the clock to bring the story to the next level, while helping me hit critical deadlines.

I'd like to thank my wife (Kelly), and my three daughters (Bailey, Olivia, and Lauren), who suffered through the emotional maelstrom that is often part of the package when you live with someone who works in the arts. They were steadfast and loving, a wonderful testimony to the amazing women that they are.

Thanks to Dean Lorey and James A. Owen, who offered encouragement when I desperately needed it.

Thank you as well to Dr. Joshua Lewis for supplying his medical knowledge, which allowed me to assassinate a fictional senator in a creative and believable manner. And to Derek Benz, whose knowledge of the cyber community's underbelly helped me understand what Tempest shielding is.

I'd also like to recognize the artists who lent their talents to this book, including Mike Dubisch, Todd Nauck, Enrique Rivera, Danny Araya, and Kyle Latino.

And very special thanks to Grey Arnold, who helped keep me on point.

ABOUT THE AUTHOR

Author photo by
Scott Mitchell

Jon S. Lewis is the coauthor of the Grey Griffins trilogy and the Grey Griffins Clockwork Chronicles. He also writes for the DC COMICS family of publishers. He resides with his family in Arizona.

visit JonSLewis.com and ChaosNovels.com